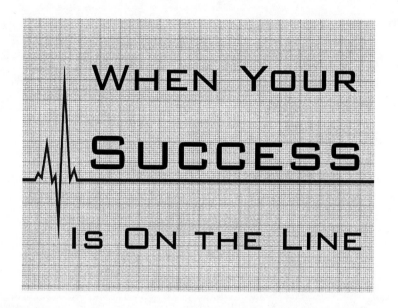

WHEN YOUR SUCCESS IS ON THE LINE

DR. WALTER WEST

PUBLISHED BY WESTVIEW, INC., NASHVILLE, TENNESSEE

PUBLISHED BY WESTVIEW, INC.
P.O. Box 210183
Nashville, Tennessee 37221
www.publishedbywestview.com

ISBN 978-1-935271-22-2 paperback
     978-1-935271-24-6 hardback

First edition, July 2009

Printed in the United States of America on acid free paper.

To my family,

Monica, Rachel, and Adam

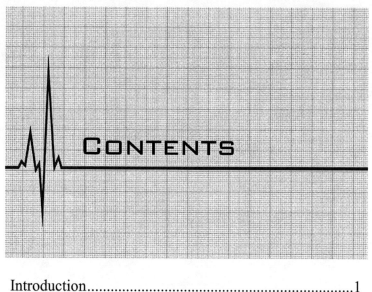

CONTENTS

INTRODUCTION

(or, What I Didn't Know about Business Could Fill a Book)

When I established my optometry practice in 1975, my entire plan could be summarized easily: I need an office, equipment, furniture, inventory, and enough patients to fill a schedule.

I was fresh out of the Southern College of Optometry, and my wife Monica and I were eager to move to Middle Tennessee and set up the practice.

Once I had the office and patients, I thought everything else would fall into place on its own. After all, I was a doctor and knew how to examine patients, prescribe medication, sell glasses, and fit contact lenses. I also understood that I needed more money coming in than going out. Unfortunately, that was about it. I had no idea of how to set my fees, determine my hours, identify my geographic market area, understand the demographics of that market area, manage my practice income, or amortize the debt associated with starting my practice. This list could go on and on.

In fact, it was only after I was in it up to my neck that I had two realizations, almost simultaneously: 1) my optometry "practice" was actually a business that required business skills to operate; and 2) I didn't have these skills.

I'm happy to say that twenty-seven years after opening the doors, our small business had grown into a multi-million dollar enterprise. Our hard work had paid off, and we were thriving. Everything seemed to be right on track.

Then everything changed.

One morning, I woke up with double vision. Medically speaking, this is a very bad sign. Brain tumor, I thought. Stroke. Aneurism.

I count myself as fortunate. After three weeks of testing, I learned it was not a life-threatening event. But the double vision remained, and I couldn't properly examine my patients. I tried to wait it out while seeking treatment.

A month passed. Then three. Soon it became clear to me that I would never again be able to practice optometry. I was done, and so was my practice.

Naturally, this was hard to accept. I was educated to practice optometry and had spent my entire professional life building a business around this set of skills. Furthermore, I enjoyed the work and believed I was good at it.

None of that mattered. I was finished as an optometrist, and I needed to find a new way to support my family.

I began to assess my situation. First, I needed to deal with my emotions — I had anger, fear, and frustration in abundance. Then, after beginning to accept what had been lost, I decided to take account of what remained.

That's when it dawned on me: I had spent my professional life learning, developing, and honing my *business* skills, just as much as I had my technical skills as an optometrist. And though I would never again be able to examine a patient, my ability to run a business was stronger than it had ever been.

During this self-examination, I realized that while I had reams of analytical documents associated with the practice of optometry, I had precious little to document the business strategies integral to the success of my practice — and I'd spent nearly three decades developing them. At this point in my life, I needed to know *exactly* what skills I still possessed so I could get myself back out in the marketplace.

I had to find a way to move forward. As a first step, I decided to map out the skills and methods I developed over the years and evaluate their worth. Once I had a clear idea of my skills and their value, I could confidently sell myself in the marketplace; and that is just what happened.

Along the way, I realized I was amassing a lot of research on what had been most important to the success of my small business. I was gathering information, much like my library of reference and medical texts — only this information was about how to operate a business, manage employees, and ignite the engine of self-motivation.

This book is a product of that research.

My purpose for writing the book is threefold.

Primarily, I want to encourage those of you who might be considering business ownership to go ahead and take the first step. Some of the greatest opportunities for achievement lie in owning your own business, and I want to provide firm footing for those brave enough to begin the journey.

Secondly, for anyone already running a small business and searching for ways to improve operations, I offer my book as guidance.

And finally, for anyone who has had your life's work taken away from you, I offer a blueprint for reassessing the value of your experience.

While this should come as no surprise, this book does not contain everything you need to know to be successful in business. What it does contain, however, is a great deal of information you're not likely to learn from formal education or on-the-job training. I hope to provide you with some of the knowledge I gained and lessons I have learned throughout my business life.

My hope is that my message and the experiences, insights, and tools that I share will pay dividends in the form of success and self-satisfaction throughout your career.

CHAPTER ONE

You've Gotta Be a Wannabe

Every business owner wants to be more than merely successful. We want our start-up businesses to quickly become known and accepted in the marketplace. We strive for consistent and ever-increasing profitability, and ultimately, we want to benefit from the successful sale of the business. But that's not all we want.

Along the way, we want our businesses to grow and attract more customers. We want to provide a higher level of service; we want to use the newest technology; and we want to work in spacious, well-appointed facilities. Not only do we plan for the start and growth of our business but also for the development of competitive advantages and strategies to protect our market share from competition — now and in the future. Our attention is on the relationships we build with our customers. We want to create the sense that we are now, and forever will be, their best and most trusted source for products and services. In essence, we are creating a standard for our customers — a standard that they can use to measure any business in any industry.

We want to be recognized as the businessmen, businesswomen, and professionals we are, and for the outstanding service and quality we offer. We want to be respected for the professional knowledge we possess and the manner in which we work with and serve our customers. We also want to be respected and recognized by our peers for who we are and what we offer our customers and our industry as a whole. We want a sense of belonging, fitting in, and being part of our industries, and we want the self-satisfaction that comes from these accomplishments.

It's Okay to Be a Wannabe

From this long list of our numerous wants and needs, it seems we are all "wannabes." It's interesting that the term *wannabe* is typically a putdown or carries a negative connotation, generally indicating that someone is acting like something he's not. Wannabes are perceived as charlatans, posers, or merely followers imitating the dress, the speaking style, the physical movements, or the behavior of those they admire. Of course, the wannabe is innocently trying to see, feel, or experience what it might be like if he were that person whom he reveres.

The old saying, "walk a mile in their shoes," reminds us that we might see or judge someone differently if we knew more about what his life was like. In many ways, wannabes are trying to walk in their idols' shoes to experience what they do. True, they haven't lived those lives themselves or accomplished what their idols or role models have accomplished, but we should all be more tolerant of the wannabes for their quest to understand and their desire to experience.

We encourage high school and university students to shadow someone who is active in the vocation or profession they're interested in pursuing. In fact, an integral part of medical training is a process whereby interns learn from and, in many ways, mimic the performance and behavior of residents; in turn, residents do the same with attending physicians and department heads in a hospital setting. Even though they are at different levels, interns and residents are wannabes.

Many businesses have formalized the mentor/protégé relationship, and they require employees to participate. Within some companies and industries, a new hire isn't allowed to interact with customers or clients until his or her mentor feels it's appropriate. When that time comes, all contact with customers or clients still initially occurs only under the watchful eye of the mentor. Mentors critique, coach, redirect, challenge, and encourage their protégés to enhance their performances so that one day they will be able to work on their own. The protégés of today will be the mentors of tomorrow. This relationship is a necessity in any business where an individual with a formal education and training requires the direction and modeling of experience to become effective, efficient, and profitable without being a liability.

I've mentioned the more formalized relationships of interns to residents and residents to attending physicians, as well as the protégé/mentor relationship. What about small business owners, who don't have these structured relationships to help them advance in their chosen fields? How do they polish their skills and gain needed experience? How do they learn what is achievable, and how do they become confident enough to set their sights higher? The answer to all of these questions is that many don't. Those who do, however, are likely perceived as wannabes because, for them, the only approach left is to try it on, and see how it feels. To do this, they need to walk, talk, eat, sleep, adopt the value systems, and behave as their role models do.

For those of you who don't have a formalized mentoring relationship available — perhaps because you are the business owner or these relationships don't exist in your industry — recognize that not all mentoring situations are positive. Unfortunately, I have seen instances where a mentoring program or relationship was stifling to the point of being counterproductive. When a mentoring program or relationship exists in a less-than-progressive industry and is used to maintain the status quo, or when the program suppresses ambition and creativity by being exclusive rather than inclusive, or when its sole purpose is to preserve the "good ole' boy network," there's nothing positive about it.

Find Your Own Way

When I began practicing optometry at age twenty-three, I was naïve and, unfortunately, I'd never heard of a mentor. One reason might be that the mentor relationship hadn't yet been popularized in leadership and management books. Another reason, although I hate to admit it, was probably because I was searching for answers more than I was searching for the *ability* to answer. Plus, at that time, a new practitioner in the market was more often seen as competition rather than a colleague.

Although no one was offering to mentor me nor inviting me to come to them with questions or concerns, this didn't seem strange. That was okay. It just meant I had to try to figure things out for myself. Often, it meant that I had to learn from my mistakes rather than having someone guide me around pitfalls to a more effective and less expensive course. As I look back, I don't have any regrets about the lack of assistance offered nor sought. In many ways, it might have been a blessing in disguise. Here's why I believe this.

In 1975, the business model for optometry had been the same for at least thirty years. By setting out to build my practice in a nontraditional fashion, I unknowingly differentiated my practice from others in the market. I developed my own ideas about the level of service that should be delivered and the expectations I wanted my patients to have for the convenience, attentiveness, and professional care they received. Without being aware of the terminology at the time, I had begun to create a customer-centric or, in my case, a patient-centric practice rather than an organization-centric or doctor-centric practice.

I began focusing on how to satisfy every patient at every visit, often meeting demands for service and convenience that at the time I didn't realize other doctors would have considered unreasonable and refused to even attempt. Certainly, there were times when I was frustrated by how much effort was required to deliver the level of quality and service I had promised. Yet, as I saw my practice grow, and patients return and refer others, I realized they weren't seeking me out because of the eye examinations I provided, or the glasses or contact lenses I sold, but rather because of the unique experience I created for each patient. Later, I understood that I was in the business of selling a satisfying experience, one patient at a time, rather than eye examinations, glasses, or contact lenses. The organization-centric or doctor-centric model offered only one type of experience. Regardless of individual wants, needs, or personal preferences, every patient was forced into the same experience. In contrast, I offered my patients the care they needed with as many different experiences as I had patients.

Always Be a Wannabe

There are businesses now that are more successful than ever. There are businesses now that are larger, have more customers, clients, or patients, and provide a higher level of service than ever before. There are businessmen and businesswomen who use the newest technology and work in facilities that are spacious and well-appointed. Many businessmen and businesswomen are recognized and respected as professionals in their own industries and others for the professional knowledge they possess and the manner in which they serve their customers. They are recognized not only for what they provide their customers individually, but also for what they offer their industry as a whole. These individuals have a well-deserved sense of belonging, and they enjoy the self-satisfaction that results from these accomplishments and more.

When I started my business I was a wannabe. Thirty-three years later, I remain so, perhaps more now than ever before. There are still things I want to accomplish, skills I want to improve or acquire, things I want to experience, places I want to go; and I pray it will always be so. We all want to be something we're not and accomplish things we haven't, and that's not a bad thing. Your business or industry is in its current state of advancement because, in the past, there were wannabes: those who envisioned more.

The business people who have accomplished these things are the current leaders, and they lead by doing, by accomplishing, by setting an example, by mentoring. In my experience, the best mentors are the most accomplished, the most successful, the most willing to share their good fortune, and the least likely to feel threatened when doing so. I find it interesting that in talking to these leaders, they all still "wannabe" more than they are. They want to accomplish more, and they are willing to share their experience.

Regardless of our individual accomplishments, it seems there's always someone who has done it bigger or better, or has taken a different approach than anyone else. To learn from them is simple; we only have to listen, follow, and always, always "wannabe."

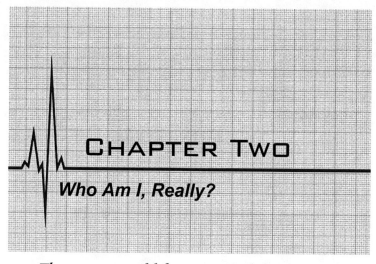

CHAPTER TWO

Who Am I, Really?

The unexamined life is not worth living. —

Socrates

I wholeheartedly agree with that bit of wisdom, and I'd like to extend the sentiment, paraphrasing it in the context of running a business: *the unexamined business will not be alive for very long.*

And the beating heart of your business is *you.*

The simple fact is that you've got to know who you are, what you want, what skills you have, and what skills you need to develop if you hope to succeed. This is your starting point, and you need to be honest with yourself while conducting this self-examination.

Consider these general questions:

* ❖ What do I want from life personally?
* ❖ What do I want from life professionally?
* ❖ What are my strengths? Weaknesses?
* ❖ What do I like? Dislike?
* ❖ How do I actually want to spend my time?
* ❖ How much am I willing to sacrifice in order to achieve my goals?
* ❖ And again, what do I really want from my life?

Try sitting down and writing out honest answers to these questions. Treat it like an assignment from your boss, and one he or she counts as critical to the success of an important project. You wouldn't put in a half-hearted attempt if your boss asked this of you, would you? Of course not, and if you did, you might not have a job for long. So what I'm suggesting to you is this: the important project upon which you are always working on is the trajectory of your career and personal life. And if you hope to succeed in this project, your chances will be greatly improved if you bring an honest and analytical approach to your research. Don't just think about the answers in your head or say them aloud; actually write your answers down. Study and expand on them. Carry this with you everywhere for a week and read it several times a day. Add to it, modify it, and eliminate from it. For this one week, work on this project as if everything else you hope to accomplish depends upon it. The knowledge gained from this self-analysis will become the foundational rock upon which you build a happy, thoughtful, and productive life.

Now, granted, answering these questions is much harder than asking them, but this process can provide a road map for moving your life to a place you want to be. Your answers will change with time, so put yourself through this exercise again and again. We all benefit from regular self-examination.

Self-Awareness Is Essential to Your Success

You have to know what you want before you set out to get it. As amazingly simple as that sounds, the fact is that many people approach their professional careers without having a clear idea of what they want out of life. They don't know because they haven't taken the time to figure out *who* they are. Granted, self-discovery is a lifelong process, and you may not even be able to know what it is you really want until you get further along. But you need to have a starting point − a place where you begin the essential research of yourself.

So what does self-knowledge have to do with running a successful business? A lot. Besides knowing what it is you want, you need to know where your strengths and weaknesses lie. You do this so you can accentuate and build upon your strengths, while improving upon and mitigating your weaknesses. For example, if you enjoy spending your time with customers and have strong customer service skills, perhaps you should focus part of your business model on providing the best customer service available. On the other hand, if you find your customer service skills lacking, perhaps you should delegate that job to someone better suited for it, or focus on this shortcoming and consciously work to improve it.

When you have a clear understanding of your own strengths and weaknesses, you're able to build a business plan that makes more sense and will make your operation more efficient. This informed business plan will save you time and money. By capitalizing on your strengths, you are actually maximizing the productivity of your central business asset – yourself. You are making hay where the haymaking is good. When you stray away from your strengths and find yourself bogged down in areas where your skills are not so strong, you are losing productivity. The principle of "penny wise and pound foolish" comes into play here. There are many times when delegating responsibility – even if that means a payroll increase – makes more sense than limiting the productivity of your primary asset. That doesn't mean you shouldn't improve upon your weaknesses. You certainly should. And if you're a small businessperson, you have to know about every aspect of your business. So if you spot a weakness in your abilities, don't ignore it. Explore and improve it, but know there are times when you must step away and delegate the responsibility. Remember, none of this analysis is possible if you don't begin by examining your strengths and weaknesses.

You also need to know your threshold for sacrifice. How much are you willing to give to your venture? Once you have an idea about what you want to achieve and what you have to achieve with, you need to figure out what will be *required* of you to get there. Try to determine what these requirements are and ask yourself if you are willing to make the personal sacrifices that go along with them.

Many people enter business without fully realizing what it will ask of them. Their enthusiasm may blind them to the demands of running a business. Or maybe they haven't really done their homework, leaving them unaware of these demands until they are made painfully obvious. You need to avoid these scenarios by being as realistic and prepared as you can possibly be. But make no mistake, you will make many personal sacrifices along the way, and you need to know how much you are willing to give up in pursuit of your professional goals and dreams.

The upshot of being aware of your personal limits of sacrifice is that you can plan and manage accordingly. So much of business — and our lives — is about knowing where we stand. If you know what has to be done and what it will take to do it, you can evaluate your business to see if you have the resources to achieve it. In small business, the central resource is usually you and your time. If your business model requires you to work sixteen-hour days for the next three years, then that is probably not a very realistic model. But if your model has you working twelve-hour days for only six months, after which you would be able to hire an assistant, you may find the sacrifice well within your limits. The key is to know where you stand and plan accordingly.

All of this "know yourself" talk may seem too touchy-feely for some people. They may think of business as a cold, hard way of making money in which you just do what has to be done. But that's not the case. Knowing yourself is about being *prepared* to meet the challenges of running a good business or living a good life. Furthermore, good businesses are built on good relationships. Customers, distributors, employees, regulating bodies, landlords, and neighbors all represent critical elements of business that are based on human relationships. Nearly everything you do in business has an underlying relationship that supports its function. Outside of the business context, we largely define ourselves according to our relationships. We want to be loving spouses, good parents, or good friends. Good relationships are the good stuff of life. They make us happy and content. And you will not realize your full potential for this good stuff unless you have a realistic idea about who you are. The first relationship we have is the one with ourselves, and it determines the quality of all the others.

Think of self-awareness as a sort of super-skill. It can define the limits and effectiveness of all of your other skills. When you enter any venture with a firm idea of what you want, what you have, and what you're willing to sacrifice to get there, then you're way ahead of the game. At that point, you have the opportunity to build and manage your business based upon a solid understanding of your assets and limitations. As you move forward in you professional career, you will also be moving forward in your personal life. What you know about yourself will change, as will your desires and needs. That's why there's really no finish line for self-discovery — it is a process. But, again, think of it as a skill, one that will improve the more you practice it. The better you get at this super-skill, the better off your business will be — and the life that business is built on.

CHAPTER THREE

Not Every Successful Businessperson Is an Entrepreneur–and That's Okay

The term *entrepreneur* is frequently used as a synonym for someone who owns his or her own business. I don't agree with this generalization. I believe this casual use of the term entrepreneur is misleading and needlessly deters many people from considering business ownership. The sum total of men and women in the business world today is much like the structure of an iceberg. Only a few – the successful and well-known entrepreneurs – are visible. Most remain anonymous, unrecognized for their achievements, even if they are just as successful as their high-profile counterparts. Using the term entrepreneur to describe any and all business owners is misleading because it gives a false impression that certain rare qualities and abilities are required to start or own a business. I know many successful, independent business owners, but I would describe very few of them as entrepreneurial. Even so, they display many of the attributes I associate with entrepreneurs.

Attributes of an Entrepreneur

Anyone who is successful in business is likely to have many of the qualities attributed to entrepreneurs. Take *innovation*. Business owners who develop fresh new ideas for their products or services are successful because they are innovative. Others possess great *initiative*. They are world-class self-starters, who are able to motivate people within their organizations. Then there are those who possess a *creativity* that is either essential or extremely advantageous in their field. Another important group are the *problem-solvers*. These individuals have an innate ability to, first, recognize that a problem exists, then find solutions and set them in motion. And I cannot forget the *hard workers*, those who are willing to put in the long hours often required to be successful in business. Finally, there are the *exceptional leaders*. They are skilled at identifying a goal and then communicating it effectively so that everyone in their organization understands and can visualize how to achieve it.

These attributes are definitely advantageous to the business owner who has them. In fact, many successful business owners possess several, if not most, of these characteristics. There's one trait, however, that I believe elevates a successful business owner to entrepreneur status, and that is the ability to be *visionary*.

The visionaries conceptualize, visualize, integrate, and communicate ideas; they then grow them into a business, products, or alternate methods of delivery or distribution. These entrepreneurs recognize opportunities that are overlooked by everyone else. Occasionally, people have expertise in one field that makes them an entrepreneur in another. It works like this: a person has a particular knowledge base or skill set that serves him well in his field. Then, as a result of advancing technology, emerging need, or industry overlap, that person recognizes and exploits an opportunity created by his area of expertise, thus establishing a niche. And *voilà!* An entrepreneur is born.

Profile of a True Entrepreneur

Entrepreneurs come from all walks of life, cultural backgrounds, and ethnicities. Many are recognized as entrepreneurs in the dawning of their business lives, while others are in their twilight when they achieve that status. Some you've never heard of, and some can be found at the tip of that iceberg for the entire world to see. There are far too many to name, even among the ones who are famous, so let's look at just one example. In addition to being an innovative self-starter, a creative problem-solver, and a leader, he is also a visionary.

Steve Jobs is someone I consider a true entrepreneur. His work with computers was innovative as well as visionary. It wasn't that computers didn't exist before Jobs came along. They did. In fact, there were some very large, very powerful (more large than powerful by today's standards) computers in existence in 1976 when Steve Jobs and Steve Wozniak founded Apple Computers, Inc. At that time, computers filled entire rooms, required special cooling, and were characterized by whirling magnetic tapes and miles of color-coded wires. They were very expensive, owned only by large institutions, and accessible to a select few, highly trained individuals. Jobs changed all of that forever with the first Apple computer. Priced at less than $700, it would fit easily on a desktop and was so simple that a child could operate it. Thanks to Jobs' innovation and vision, computers became affordable, understandable, and personal. It was Jobs, the entrepreneur, who first made computers available to the masses, and in doing so, changed the public's interest in and use of computers forever.

Jobs was also an innovator in the area of animation and computer graphics with Pixar, Inc. Pixar has produced the animated films *Toy Story, Finding Nemo, The Incredibles,* and many more. Of course, full-length animated features existed before the creation of Pixar. The Walt Disney company was the industry leader. However, through his innovative and visionary leadership, Jobs took animation to a level of sophistication and realism never before seen. Animated feature films – and the industry that produces them – have been changed forever.

Next, Jobs turned his attention to the music industry. While other forms of portable music storage and players existed, he introduced the iPod. Millions and millions of iPods later, the music industry still does not know if this invention will save or destroy it. The amazing public acceptance of this technological innovation has created a music delivery and storage method that has outpaced the recording industry's ability to manage its products.

Qualities You *Won't* Find in Entrepreneurs

Just as I associate certain attributes with entrepreneurs, there are some I can't imagine finding among them. For example, I'd never expect a true entrepreneur to be a procrastinator. True entrepreneurs have the ability to make good decisions in less time, with less discussion and fewer meetings. They rarely look back as they move on to the next challenge or decision. Because they don't tolerate indecision within their businesses, entrepreneurs hire, inspire, and lead to avoid it. I'm not implying that they're reckless or lack the discipline to consider all options: they simply consider their options and have enough confidence in their decisions to move ahead.

Entrepreneurs are not distracted from their goals, sidetracked by details, or unsure of their purpose or actions. Many business owners, CEOs, and high-level managers convolute their management structure, complicate the decision-making process, and distance themselves from the soul of their businesses. However, entrepreneurs focus on how to simplify an existing process, eliminate needless processes, and delegate responsibility to capable employees.

As an independent consultant, I enjoy a challenge and become intrigued by the unknown. I like to move quickly into action, and I'm rarely, if ever, willing to abide by inefficient procedures. I like to think of myself as entrepreneurial. My consulting takes me into many areas within many businesses, and much of my work is in marketing and communications. Although I'm often called to act as a facilitator, I also help with project development and implementation. I've noticed that when I come into contact with the corporate structure, life changes. It becomes more complicated to develop concepts, collaborate, make decisions, and move projects to completion. Every business I've worked with could benefit by stepping back from "the way we do things" in order to objectively identify policies, programs, or protocols that are inefficient — and eliminate them. Regardless of their size, many businesses could run more efficiently with greater impact and bottom line profit if the owners, CEOs, or managers were more entrepreneurial.

In an effort to improve their organizations, many independent business owners and CEOs of large corporations tend to innovate or add something new — when eliminating part of what already exists might be more effective. It's a matter of perspective, a matter of vision, a matter of knowing how you want your organization to look and behave. I'll share a story I've told many clients over the years that demonstrates this in the simplest way.

The Duck-Carver's Lesson

Shelbyville, Tennessee, is recognized as the home of the annual Tennessee Walking Horse Celebration, but years ago, it was known as the Pencil City. Pencil manufacturers were drawn to Shelbyville by the abundance of red cedar that grew locally. Red cedar is a perfect wood for making pencils because of its soft and consistent texture, which also makes it a favorite among those who carve or whittle.

As was the case in much of rural America, Saturday mornings in Shelbyville brought people to town; some came to socialize, others to shop or settle accounts with merchants, who extended credit for everything from groceries to clothing to hardware. In Shelbyville, there were also those who came to the courthouse square to whittle. They came with their pocketknives and enough wood to keep them busy until late in the afternoon. Young children would stand for hours as they watched large, rough hands delicately move the shining blades through the soft wood.

One of the regulars at the courthouse square was an older gentleman known for his ability to carve lifelike duck decoys. There were always children among the onlookers, and it was common for boys of six or seven years of age to have pocketknives of their own and want to try their hand at whittling alongside the older men. Intrigued by the duck decoys he had seen the man carve week after week, one young boy approached an older gentleman and asked if he would teach him to carve a duck. While sitting quietly next to the older gentleman, he was shown how to hold his knife and how to safely move the blade through his piece of wood. Then came the instructions from the master carver of the duck decoys: "Now, young fellow, the way you carve a duck is this. You take your block of wood in one hand and your pocketknife in the other. Very carefully start your knife into the wood, always moving it away from you, and let the shavings fall to the ground. Just keep doing that until you've cut away all of the wood that doesn't look like a duck."

After I tell this story, almost everyone's first tendency is to smile at the kindness in the story, then laugh at the simplicity of the message. And then they laugh again at the thought that something so simple could be worthy of consideration by someone in their lofty position. And yes, they shake their heads because, as their consultant, I thought it was important for them to hear. Then the insightful truth of this simple message sinks in: businesses are just as often successful because of what they aren't as what they are.

Although you don't have to be a "tip of the iceberg" business guru or overnight success story to be a flourishing business owner, employing the attributes found among entrepreneurs at any level greatly enhances your potential for success and self-satisfaction.

CHAPTER FOUR

Finding the Leader Within

I'm sure you've heard the comment that someone is a "born leader." But I don't buy it. From what I've seen, leadership is not a trait with which people are born. In some instances, individuals work hard to earn leadership positions, while in others, leadership is thrust upon on them. If you asked a group of people to name the business leaders they know, and then you assembled these leaders, you'd find that their abilities, qualities, and characteristics would vary significantly, even though they all are perceived as leaders by their followers.

The ability to lead is a product of two things: talent and skill. Although talent is God-given and can't be taught, it can be enhanced. Skills, on the other hand, can be taught, learned, and enhanced. In my experience, the strictly talented and the strictly skilled leaders are not necessarily the best leaders. The best leaders are those who have some talent and have dedicated themselves to developing and honing the skills that enable them to apply those talents more effectively. Whether or not you believe you are a leader, whether you rate yourself a good leader or an average leader, whether you believe your leadership ability comes from talent or from skills that you've learned, you will recognize that all good leaders have some characteristics and abilities in common.

If you research leadership, you'll find tens of thousands of references. Almost everyone who has ever written about leadership has a list of the characteristics or qualities of a good leader. And yes, I have my list, too. Something I know for sure as you read my list is that you will think it's incomplete, or you will believe I've listed characteristics that shouldn't be there. The list of characteristics someone assigns to a leader varies from individual to individual. It's not so much what the leader has to offer: it's what the followers are looking for; and it's not so much what the leader accomplishes, but what those around him accomplish.

Another common aphorism is, "There are leaders, and there are followers." I believe there's a third group – those who merely fall into line. What's the difference between a follower and someone who falls into line? The follower first has to be a believer. Followers are behind you because they understand the vision you communicate to them, and their description of success is the same as yours. Whereas, those who just fall into line may blindly follow you without ever truly understanding your goal or how they'll benefit by reaching it.

It's not the title *leader*, but the quality of leadership that makes an individual stand out from others. In my mind, leadership is associated with people who are assertive in their speech and their actions. They are purposeful. At the same time, good leaders have compassion for their employees. They know how to handle pressure and use it as a stimulus, as opposed to a hindrance to progress. Most importantly, good leaders recognize that their role is to serve their followers, rather than have their followers serve them.

Good leaders are most likely to be needed – and recognized – during times of change, when a business may be unstable and characterized by confusion. During this change, employees may be fearful. Productivity may drop, and employees may lack a clear understanding of the direction in which the business is going. During times of change, emotions can run high, with employees longing for what used to be and struggling to understand what lies ahead. A good leader can calm their fears and ensure employees that the business is moving in the proper direction. Good leaders clarify the business's new goals (and rewards) and communicate them in a way that helps unite the workforce. While some leaders have what I call the "Lone Ranger leadership mentality" and try to do everything themselves, the most effective leaders help create other leaders within the organization.

Success in leadership is not an all-or-nothing proposition. The level of success varies from one leader to the next. As you begin to take inventory of your leadership ability, attributes, talents, and skills, don't be discouraged if you recognize shortfalls. There are always opportunities to improve, and the first step toward improvement is an awareness of the need to do so.

Characteristics of a Leader

An exemplary character is of the utmost importance for a leader. I encourage you to take note of the following traits that comprise exemplary character and decide if you have a particular talent, certain skills, or the need to develop in these areas. As I mentioned, everyone's list of good leadership characteristics will vary, so feel free to add the traits that you feel are most appropriate to you.

- ❖ *Trustworthiness* is critical for anyone in a leadership role. Leaders must be honest in all things and never participate in deception.

- ❖ Leaders must be *reliable*. Those who follow you must know you will do what you say, even when it's difficult or unpopular.

- ❖ Leaders must have the *courage* to make tough decisions and do the right thing in difficult circumstances, even when no one is watching.

- ❖ Your employees must recognize your *loyalty* to them and know that you will stand by them. They must know that, although you will hold them responsible for their performance, you will do so in a forthright manner.

- ❖ You must treat everyone in your organization with *respect*. The Golden Rule, "Do unto others as you would have them do unto you," certainly applies here.

- ❖ As a leader, you must be *tolerant* of differences among your employees. If you have an organization with fifty employees, you need to treat them as fifty individuals, not as a single unit.

❖ You need to be *sensitive* to the feelings of others, and have empathy or sympathy for those in your organization.

❖ You must take *responsibility* for yourself and your actions, and always consider the consequences, not only personal ones but those for the other individuals in your organization.

❖ You must be *accountable* for your choices. Good or bad, you have to own them either way.

❖ Leaders must have a sense of *fairness.* If guidelines are set down that everyone is to observe, then the leader must follow them, too. The leader must be willing to hear grievances with an open mind, gain insight about those grievances, and be able to communicate an understanding of others' feelings.

❖ Good leaders must have *compassion.* Those you lead must know that you care about their best interests and will do what's right in all cases, not just what's best for you.

❖ Good leaders focus on *purposeful action* with a goal or an accomplishment in mind.

❖ Leaders have to be *accessible* and *approachable* by those who follow. In fact, good leaders recognize that some of the best opportunities to improve their leadership result from listening to followers describe how things could be improved.

❖ The best leaders are *assertive* and *positive* in action, and solution-focused rather than problem-focused.

❖ A leader must have a clear sense of *self-awareness*, which comes from regularly taking a personal inventory of abilities and potential limitations.

❖ A good leader makes a *commitment* to the satisfactory completion of a goal.

❖ Good leaders have *confidence* that their followers are capable and willing to dispatch their responsibilities in a timely manner. In addition, they must be able to inspire confidence in their employees and help them become the best that they can be, while recognizing that each person is unique.

❖ Good leaders must be *enthusiastic* and able to communicate their enthusiasm in a manner that is infectious within their organizations.

❖ Leaders must be able to *motivate* their followers. This motivation may stem from recognition, compensation, or from clearly communicating the potential positive or negative results associated with accomplishing or falling short of a goal.

❖ Leaders are *visionaries.* They have the ability to see what is and conceptualize what could be, while communicating their vision effectively so others can appreciate the opportunity.

❖ Leaders must be *good communicators.*

The last quality on my list is the most important by far. Communication skills are the foundation of great leadership. The reason is simple. An individual can possess all of the leadership characteristics I've listed, but if he can't communicate effectively, the potential impact of any of the other characteristics is significantly limited. Good communication skills are the key for establishing and nurturing good business and personal relationships. Lacking these relationships, a leader's effectiveness will be significantly reduced, if not lost altogether.

When we think of good communication skills, we typically think of how we speak with others. The leader must be able to communicate assertively and focus on solutions rather than problems, with a confident and honest voice, while conveying passion and commitment. Perhaps the most important communication skill for good leaders is the ability to listen. Not just sit as words bounce off of their eardrums, but *actively* listen: making good eye contact, interacting with the speaker, asking questions for clarification, and understanding not only the facts but also the emotions involved in what's being communicated. Leaders also must recognize that actions speak louder than words. Some of the most effective leaders communicate the best by setting an example. (For more on how to communicate like a leader, see Chapter Five.)

Every leader has a unique approach to his or her employees. Consistency is important. Radically changing your personal style will confuse those who have followed you to this point. Certainly, you can enhance your leadership skills and put new skills into action as your relationships with your employees grow. Just be mindful that while you're growing in your leadership role, your followers will need to adapt as much as you do, if not more.

Build on What You Have

How do you become a leader or improve your leadership skills? Well, you don't have to be over six feet tall. You don't have to be well-spoken or eloquent in front of an audience. You don't have to have that something special that no one can ever seem to define, and you don't have to be born a leader.

First, you must want to become a leader (or a better leader.) Next, you must recognize that you're not looking for followers, but rather, your employees are looking for someone in whom they can place their trust. They're looking for someone who is working for the greater good of the business and for the greater good of the individual employees as well. They're looking for someone they not only *will* follow, but also, and more importantly, *want to* follow.

You don't become a leader until you have followers who first believed in you, trusted you, and elevated you to that role. Their trust in you and their belief that you trust them has put you in the leadership role. You must clearly communicate in every way possible that you recognize you're not accomplishing anything by yourself but rather through the efforts of those who follow. You must acknowledge your employees' accomplishments and always deflect credit in their direction. In addition, you must understand and clearly state your convictions. You don't lead employees by focusing on statistics, charts, dashboards, quotas, or forecasts. You lead employees by focusing on the people.

To begin developing as a leader, you need to discover exactly who and what you are. How can you do this? Take a brutally honest personal inventory. Compare your traits with those listed above. Ask a trusted friend for an unbiased opinion. And don't be discouraged if you feel you fall short. Consider those traits that you do possess as advantages, and those that are lacking as opportunities.

Once you've gone through this discovery process and started to implement what you've learned about becoming a leader, you may expect to see immediate improvement in your business. You won't. Becoming a leader is not an event. It's a process, a journey on which you will grow. As you grow as a leader, so will the lives you touch. It's only after your followers grow that you'll see improvement in your business.

CHAPTER FIVE

Eye Contact
and a Firm Handshake . . .
Now What?

Whether it's in business or personal relationships, we've all been warned: you don't get a second chance to make a good first impression. During the first fifteen seconds of your initial interaction with a stranger, he or she begins to form an opinion of you. These new acquaintances appraise your behavior, as well as your appearance from head to toe. They observe your demeanor, your mannerisms, and your body language. They even notice your grooming and your accessories — your watch, handbag, briefcase, and shoes (and whether those shoes are shined!)

Not everyone's first impression of you will be the same, but the first impression process occurs in every new meeting. Either consciously or subconsciously, people are looking for clues as to whether or not they want to spend more time with you. Once that first impression is made, it's irreversible.

Personal Measuring Stick

Here's how these first-impression scenarios usually play out: if the person you're meeting senses that both of you are in comparable business positions or social levels, or if it seems you're both interested in similar activities, sports, or hobbies, then it's likely you'll be perceived as someone with whom they'd like to have further interaction and conversation. If it appears you're at a higher business or social level, the individual may admire you and proactively cultivate a relationship because you could be a valuable contact or asset. If, however, you are judged to be in a lower business position or social standing, you may be tolerated but not completely involved in the conversation by some of those interacting with you. Although it may seem unfair, and in some cases inappropriate, it's completely natural for people to make these appraisals.

With this universally recognized need to instantly present the "best you" possible, many people become anxious, nervous, or fearful — and as a result, present anything but their best attributes. What's more, feeling as though your first impression was not a good one may make you even more self-conscious the next time you meet a new person. I'd like to share some great techniques for creating that all-important positive first impression. But first, I want to discuss some communication basics — listening and speaking.

What Is Your Listening Style?

The best way to make a positive first impression is to make the other person the center of interest and conversation. Spend too much time talking about yourself and you may lose great opportunities to develop friendships, open job opportunities, and network. Demonstrating your interest in the other person will help ensure that first-time acquaintances will look forward to seeing you again.

One way to keep the conversation centered on the other person is to ask questions and then listen. I know this sounds simple, but the ability to listen attentively to others doesn't seem to come easily to some. In fact, listening is a skill that most people haven't recognized as one that deserves active training, practice, and development. It seems all of us could be better listeners, but we don't develop the skill because we don't grasp how important it is to our overall success.

I group individuals into four basic listening styles. In the first group are the *passive* listeners. These are the people I refer to as the "bumps on the pickle." They're there, but they serve no apparent purpose. Passive listeners generally make eye contact with the speaker, although not consistently. They generally don't show much emotion with their facial expressions, gestures, or body language. They nod their heads occasionally as though they understand, and every once in a while, they acknowledge the speaker with an "uh-huh."

Others use a *selective* approach to listening, although "listening" may not be totally accurate. Instead of listening, these individuals are merely waiting for their turn to speak. Often, their facial expressions and body language indicate they're disinterested. A selective listener tends to check his watch, flip through papers, and look around the room to see who else has entered. It's not so much that selective listeners are listening to parts of what you say. They're actually listening for you to mention a topic that they're interested in, so they can change the direction of the conversation toward that topic. Selective listeners change topic and direction by beginning to speak or by asking questions that lead to their area of interest.

The *attentive* style of listening is much preferred over the first two. These individuals typically make steady eye contact with the speaker. Their facial expressions and their body language show they're interested. They nod to indicate that they understand, and they interject, "Okay. I see. That's interesting." They also tend to ask questions that allow you to provide more information or greater detail.

While being an attentive listener will enhance your first impressions and your ability to converse well, there's another, even better approach — the *active* listening style. Active listeners make steady eye contact and project patience with their facial expressions and body language. Not only do they give you verbal feedback, such as, "I see. Yes, that's interesting," but they ask questions and make comments to let you know they're interested and they understand the feelings and emotions attached to the story being told. The active listener is also good about asking questions for clarification, as opposed to asking questions in a confrontational manner.

In my role as a consultant, I meet over a thousand new people every year in professional and social settings. While most people make favorable first impressions, some completely miss the mark. At a recent dinner, I saw examples of first-impression extremes. I sat at a table with six colleagues, and two of them failed to make a good first impression with me — or anyone else. One didn't interact at all. His passive listening failed to indicate he cared or understood the topic of discussion. The other failed to make a good first impression because he regaled us with his life story, barely giving anyone else an opportunity to enter the conversation. He used the selective listening style and constantly turned the conversation back to areas in which he was interested.

To keep things in perspective, be aware that if you're meeting someone for the first time, not only are you concerned about *his* first impression of *you*, but, also, he's thinking about *your* first impression of *him*. Both of you are doing this first impression dance at the same time. The better your listening skills, the more you'll be able to allow the other individual to lead in this first-impression dance. The one who leads will then feel that the attention has been on him, and therefore, he is more likely to want to visit with you again.

Just as I've told you there are four listening styles, there are also four styles of speaking. These speaking styles, one of which you'll recognize as your own, have a great impact on any first impression.

What Is Your Speaking Style?

The first speaking style I'll discuss is the *nonassertive* style. Nonassertive speakers typically speak in a very soft voice. They tend to take a more passive role in conversations. Eye contact is often lacking, and body language and posture indicate a submissive attitude, which, by default, puts the other speaker in a more dominant position.

Nonassertive speakers come across as lacking self-confidence and are very wishy-washy in a conversation. They typically won't express their points of view, yet will agree with everyone else's. Nonassertive speakers also tend to ramble during a conversation, seeming as if they will never get to the point. Often, their message is preceded and followed by statements that reduce or discount the validity of the statement. An example of this would be, "I hope you don't mind me saying this, it's only my opinion, and I may not be right. In fact, I'm not really even sure. Well, okay, what I think is maybe it would be a good idea to extend the hours of operation. Like I said, it's only my opinion, and it may not be right. I hope you didn't mind my making the suggestion."

As I'm sure you recognized, this speaking style generates a whole lot of talk and not a lot of message. Because of this, it's often difficult to listen to nonassertive speakers. They make listeners anxious, and in the end, listeners realize that nothing has really been communicated.

Next is the *aggressive* style of speaking. Aggressive speakers often raise their voices, sometimes use harsh language, and may be confrontational or challenging. They tend to come across as hostile, controlling, or manipulative, and they are quick to place blame and find fault. They typically demonstrate intimidating body language, such as finger-pointing or pounding a fist into the palm of the other hand. This is the classic in-your-face style of speaking. Although aggressive speakers may try to tone down their approach when they first meet someone, they ultimately get emotionally involved in a topic and show their true colors.

The next speaking style is the *passive-aggressive* style. The primary tool these individuals use is sarcasm. Their words say that they agree with you, but their tone says they do not. Their words are a put-down, but their tone says they're just joking. Passive-aggressive speakers tend to come across as condescending, and they may add body language like rolling their eyes, shaking their head, or throwing up their hands. These are often the people who, rather than communicate directly to you about some difficulty they have, will go over you to a superior or speak to colleagues about you behind your back.

The speaking style that I find most effective, most enjoyable, and most appreciated is the *assertive* speaking style. Interestingly, one key characteristic of assertive speakers is how they listen. Before assertive speakers ever speak, they actively listen in the manner described earlier. Assertive speakers focus more on the solution to a problem than the fact that a problem exists. Rather than try to place blame like passive-aggressive speakers, assertive speakers gather everyone together to see how to solve the problem as a team.

Assertive speakers project confidence in their voice, body language, and gestures. They make good eye contact and use facial expressions along with their tone of voice to convey emotion while speaking. When assertive speakers have something to say, they say it to you, not whisper behind your back. They speak clearly and to the point, using language that's constructive rather than destructive.

Another important characteristic of assertive speakers is that when a problem does exist, they speak about the problem, not about the people involved. The assertive speaker is also the one who takes initiative. If there's something that needs to be discussed, the assertive speaker is the one who will get the ball rolling. The assertive speaker is the person who can make things happen.

Next to consider are some specific points that will enhance your ability to make not just a good first impression, but a good lasting impression that will help you continue to build relationships.

Respect Personal Space

Several years ago at the University of California, Los Angeles, Dr. Albert Moravian conducted a behavioral study in which he was able to determine what percentages of communication were delivered by the words spoken, by the speaker's tonal quality, and by the speaker's body language. He found that 55% of what we communicate is conveyed through our body language and 38% is expressed by our tonal quality, leaving only 7% of the total communication left to the actual words we speak.

Chances are, when you think about making a first impression, you think more about what you will say than how you will say it. With Dr. Moravian's study in mind, and recognizing that 93% of what we communicate is nonverbal, I want to turn to some topics specifically related to nonverbal communication.

First, let's take a look at where we position ourselves when we communicate with another person. In 1959, Dr. Edward Hall coined the term *proxemics* to describe certain set distances between people as they interact:

- ❖ Public space is between twelve feet and twenty-five feet from another individual.
- ❖ Social space is between four feet and twelve feet from another individual.
- ❖ Personal space is from four feet to as close as eighteen inches.
- ❖ Intimate space is closer than eighteen inches.

At fifteen feet, it's perfectly natural to wave to friends and wish them a good day in a voice loud enough for them to hear. When chatting with a small group of people at a party or some other social gathering, you're probably between four feet and twelve feet from the other individuals. Once you've begun to build a relationship with someone, your one-on-one conversations usually take place between eighteen inches and four feet. Intimate space should be reserved for just that – intimate relationships.

What about eye contact? One of the first recommendations you'll hear when trying to improve your communication skill is to make eye contact. But how much eye contact is enough, and can you overdo eye contact? Here's what works well for me. While the other person is speaking, I make eye contact 100% of the time. While I'm speaking, I make eye contact about 70% of the time. The reason for varying eye contact as you speak is to avoid literally staring someone down. If you maintain eye contact too long, people become uncomfortable and may look away. When they look away, you've just taken a dominant role in that conversation. When you're focusing on making a good first impression or trying to develop a long-term relationship, it's important that you balance the dominance scales to put the relationship on even footing.

Is This Funny?

Many people try to use humor to make a good first impression. Public speakers may tell a joke or a funny story at the beginning of a presentation to build rapport with the audience. Be very cautious about using humor. One of the main reasons that I offer this word of caution is that not all of you are funny (and you know who you are). Unless humor and the ability to sense timing comes naturally to you, don't force yourself into the uncomfortable position of trying to tell a joke or a humorous story and being concerned about whether it will be accepted. If you do put yourself in this position, your listeners will more likely respond to your anxiety than to your joke.

Know How to Disagree

Sooner or later in any conversation, someone will discuss something with which you disagree. Creating a confrontational situation can destroy any rapport that you've begun to build. Before you challenge someone's statement, you must already have built some value into a relationship and established some credibility with the other person. In fact, I recommend that you not challenge the other individual as wrong; instead, offer another viewpoint and always acknowledge that you might be wrong. When you acknowledge that you might be wrong, use an assertive tone of voice to avoid this being perceived as a sign of weakness.

Dress for Respect

Marketers know from years of experience that the way you package a product has a lot to do with how that product is perceived and whether or not it's accepted in the marketplace. Fair or not, your first impression has a lot to do with how you package yourself – meaning the way you dress.

Although the standards for appropriate business and social attire have changed over the years, the insight I'll share on dressing is this: the way you dress shows the person you're meeting how important you believe he is. For example, if I show up for a meeting wearing a sport coat and tie and the other person is wearing blue jeans and an open-collar shirt, the message that I receive is that the opportunities I might be presenting are not necessary or important. Whenever you're not sure about appropriate dress for any occasion, it's best to err on the side of formality.

Don't Be Perfect

In trying to build a good first impression, it's important to be a little less than perfect. You might think the closer to perfection you are, the more apt you are to attract others and entertain them in conversation. However, you want to be careful not to praise yourself and your virtues to the point of boring the other individual. Recognize that it's not perfection that will attract others, but rather some of your faults and inconsistencies that make you more human, more interesting, and more approachable.

But What Do I Say?

The topics you choose to discuss have a lot to do with the first impression you create. Avoid putting up barriers by whining or complaining about problems or difficult times that you've had in your life. Avoid casting yourself in the role of the victim or the poor, depressed, misunderstood soul. Instead, strive to be positive and optimistic. A constant stream of complaints and unnecessary drama are not attractive attributes when developing a first impression.

It's Not Just Where You Stand, but How You Stand

Because 55% of what you communicate is with your body language, your posture tells a great deal to those you're trying to impress. Good posture shows confidence, whereas slouching or standing with your arms folded across your chest sends a message that you're insecure, detached from the conversation, or disinterested.

Bow Out Gracefully

Just as there's a beginning to every first impression, there's also an ending. In closing an initial conversation, it's important to let the other person know you had a good time. With a pleasant facial expression and definite eye contact, offer your hand for a shake and close with something simple like, "I'm glad we met. I've enjoyed visiting with you. I look forward to this opportunity again in the future."

Your Skills Will Evolve

In this chapter, I've discussed some of the variables involved in making a good first impression and offered some communication skills to keep the conversations flowing. This general discussion will get you started, but there's more information to learn and more study opportunities for each and every one of the variables I've mentioned. Look for pertinent resources in bookstores and online. Additional study, additional practice, and additional implementation are the only ways to get better at making first impressions.

CHAPTER SIX

The Big Idea

I often think of Benjamin Franklin as one of our country's greatest idea men. Over the course of his life, he tamed destructive storms with his lightning rod, signed all four documents critical to America's independence, and helped solidify the American character through his *Poor Richard's Almanac.* To say that he lived a prolific and productive life would be to shortchange an American genius.

Of all of his accomplishments and admirable qualities, I'd like to focus on how Benjamin Franklin, the quintessential Idea Man, continually generated so many good ideas. (Granted, they weren't all good ideas, but Franklin was not afraid of failure. In his eyes, a failure merely put him one step closer to success.)

It seems that at the foundation of Franklin's Herculean ability to generate new ideas was his disinterest in assumptions and a rejection of *fixed conclusions*. The whole world might have concluded that lightning was a force of nature that could not be harnessed. But Franklin didn't buy it. It's as though he approached everything in life with this thought in his head: "There's got to be a better way."

I would encourage you to regularly examine your business with that thought in your head. Operating your business, or managing your life, based on conclusions that you refuse to reexamine will rob you of the ability to stay nimble and thus maximize your potential.

Here's an example of how it can blow up in your face. You work hard researching for a new strategy in your business. From your research, you draw conclusions (naturally enough.) Next you make decisions and implement plans based on those conclusions, and you are successful in your efforts. That's how it should work. But here lies the danger: the underlying factors that led to your conclusions are always in flux. You don't see them. You've done the work and found success, so you are hesitant to change your conclusions. Having become attached to the conclusions that led to your success, you don't want to let them go. The next thing you know, the only research that seems valid to you is the research that supports your now *fixed* conclusions. It's a sort of positive feedback loop that can have very negative consequences.

Neither Rain, nor Sleet, nor Hail . . .

There's a longstanding approach to business that can be summarized like this:

- ❖ If it ain't broke, don't fix it;
- ❖ If it works, do more of it;
- ❖ If doesn't work, stop doing it.

While this seems like good, plain horse sense, it is actually a model for building a clunky, unresponsive business that's not likely to be progressive or strong very long. The underlying problem with this approach to business is that it allows for *the conclusions to be fixed*.

Consider this example. In 1768, when Benjamin Franklin was postmaster general to the Colonies, he made a trip to England and met with the Colonial Board of Customs. The board had a problem and sought Franklin's advice. It seems that, for some unknown reason, it took the British mail ships two weeks longer to sail from England to New York than it took merchant ships to travel from England to Newport, Rhode Island. To confound matters even further, the merchant ships that left from London had to sail down the Thames River and then across the length of the English Channel before they even reached the Atlantic Ocean. The mail ships sailed from Cornwall, which is located on the westernmost tip of England.

While this had been going on for several years, the issue was not being addressed. It seems an obvious inefficiency, so why didn't the British government correct it? Well, technically, the mail service *wasn't broken*: the mail got where it was going, so, there was nothing to fix. To the British government, *it worked*, so they kept doing more of it. Perhaps they were waiting for the system to *stop working* altogether and only then look for a solution.

It seemed obvious to Franklin that something was amiss. He began to research the problem by asking questions of experts. His cousin, a whaling captain named Timothy Folger, was in England at the time, so Franklin invited him to dinner to discuss the discrepancy. Folger was not surprised by this information. As a Nantucket whaler, he knew exactly why it was taking the mail ships longer. There was a strong easterly current at the latitude the British mail ships crossed the Atlantic that was so subtle, even the most experienced sailor would not be able to detect it. However, American whalers had been telling the

English captains how to sail around it for years. They knew this to be possible thanks to the experience and knowledge accumulated over generations, but the captains of the mail ships wouldn't listen.

"They were too wise to be counseled by simple American fisherman," Folger reportedly told his cousin. Here we find their fixed conclusion: British sea captains knew best. Furthermore, the delivery system was functional; the mail was indeed being delivered. But at what cost to efficiency?

Franklin set out to scientifically assess the situation. He'd been interested in the ocean currents for some time and now the noted polymath would attempt to prove to the English that there was indeed a better way. He began his research on the return voyage to America, drawing buckets of water samples all along the way, measuring temperatures, and recording his findings. Once back home, he began interviewing whalers for their insight. They must've been honored to have such a prestigious man seeking their advice. They told Franklin what they knew and put their logs completely at his disposal.

In 1770, Franklin published a map of the ocean current, which he named the Gulf Stream; the British largely ignored it. They maintained their belief that British sea captains knew best. It would take many years before these "superior" captains would see the error of their ways and recognize the effect of their flawed, fixed conclusion.

I love this example because of its simple elegance. So much inefficiency based upon such a poor and unfounded conclusion. The problem was glaringly obvious. Yet the British captains ignored the advice of captains more familiar with the waters, as well as ignoring the simple fact that the merchant ships were basically lapping them on the Atlantic. The message here is clear: don't let fixed conclusions cloud your judgment or your business decisions.

Fixed Conclusions Blind Us to Innovation

In the last example, we saw how fixed conclusions can cause obvious inefficiencies in a business operation. But there is another, less obvious casualty of a closed-minded approach to problem solving: innovation. Let's take another example from our Idea Man.

Ben Franklin required glasses to see at a distance. As he aged, he needed glasses to read as well and found himself in a situation many of us are familiar with – forever searching for his reading glasses.

"I therefore had, formerly, two pairs of spectacles, which I shifted occasionally, as in traveling I sometimes read, and often wanted to regard the prospects," Franklin is quoted as saying. So he wanted to read *and* be able to take in the sights as he went down the road. There was a longstanding solution to that problem: switch pairs of glasses. To make this easier, you might tie one pair around your neck. But Franklin didn't accept that solution, though switching from one pair to the other technically solved the problem.

There had to be a better way.

"Finding the change troublesome, and not always sufficiently ready, I had the glasses cut and half of each kind associated in the same [frame]," he wrote a friend. "By this means, as I wear my spectacles constantly, I have only to move my eyes up or down, as I want to see distinctly far or near, the proper glass being always ready."

Franklin had invented bifocals – a simple, elegant innovation that has improved the lives of hundreds of millions of people since its introduction. So, what was it about Franklin that allowed him to see solutions to problems that weren't even recognized as problems? It was his rejection of fixed conclusions. He wasn't constrained by society's assumption that glasses could only be manufactured to suit one particular need. He needed two sets of lenses, but only wanted to wear one pair of glasses. So, he thought of a simple solution: combine both sets of lenses in one pair of frames. This was a difficult task for the manufacturer of the glasses as it was a new process. But once the faulty assumption was out of the way, the technical challenges were overcome. Franklin would have what he called his "double spectacles."

The bottom line is that these fixed conclusions, or assumptions, about your business model and operations can stifle the growth and success of your company. You can end up with massive inefficiencies or overlook potential innovations that could advance your business significantly. Perhaps you conclude your customer service methods are all well and good, meanwhile ignoring a repeated customer complaint about ease of service. Maybe your billing system has always worked just fine, but a technology upgrade would improve accounting and save expenditures. The fact is, in a rapidly evolving business environment, a successful business owner must always be questioning these fixed conclusions and always thinking, "There's got to be a better way." Once you get the assumptions and fixed conclusions out of the way, you're able to begin solving the problem. Going forward I'll share some techniques for exploring and generating your own problem-solving ideas.

Idea Generating Techniques

While there are many techniques for idea generation, the best one is the one that works for you. It's all about structuring your thinking process and using methods that take you outside of your typical approach and safely away from the status quo. Not every method will be right for you, or even for a particular situation, but you'll likely benefit if you have a few different techniques to employ. Naturally, the more you practice these techniques, the better you'll become at using them to effectively develop ideas that will ultimately lead you to solutions. Below I've given you a few methods for generating ideas, and each of them can be used individually or in a group setting. Certainly there are many ways to generate ideas, but here are a few basic techniques I think would be a good place to start.

Brainstorming – We are all familiar with this concept, but I have often seen it used poorly. The key to brainstorming is to have two absolute rules in place. The first is to not evaluate the ideas during the session, and the second is to not assign ownership of an idea to the person who came up with it. The goal is to make the creative process completely open, and if you violate either of these rules, that won't happen. If you begin evaluating ideas while you're still in the brainstorming process, you will effectively stifle the creativity from that point forward. You don't want to burden a participant with ownership of an idea because this sometimes discourages them from offering additional ideas within the session. You want a completely open and free exchange of ideas while brainstorming. Once you've compiled all of the ideas that have been generated, you can begin the evaluation process.

Reversal/Flipping – Using this method, the participants take a given problem and reverse the premise. For example, let's say you own an auto repair shop and find that you're losing market share to the new business down the road. While performing your due diligence and analyzing your company's operations, you realize that your advertising package is outdated and the ad budget is much smaller than the industry average. So you ask yourself, "How can I put a better package together and more effectively reach my target audience?" With the reversal method, you flip that question on its head and ask, "How can I get the *worst* advertising together and then put it in front of the *wrong* market?" Okay, let's try to answer these questions. You could design the graphics yourself, even though you've never done it before. Then you could spend less money on marketing and leaflet car windshields in another part of town. Now that you know the worst you could do, let's work backward from there. Perhaps, it's time to hire a professional graphics designer, instead of having your nephew (who is good with computers) design for you. Maybe it's time to buy some ad space in the local paper. Sure, the long-term contract with the auto trader magazine is inexpensive, but it isn't bringing new customers to your shop. The key to the reversal method is all about gaining a different perspective on the problem to get your creative juices flowing.

This method can also work well in the context of a brainstorming session. Picture this: you've called your staff in for a morning meeting to brainstorm on the worst possible solutions to customer service problems. The ridiculous nature of the premise and the ideas generated from the session are sure to bring some laughter, which can be very productive, since humor is a great way to loosen up participants and really get the ideas rolling. But remember the two ground rules for brainstorming: no evaluation until the session is over, and no one owns the ideas. Now that you've got your list of bad ideas together, reverse them and work backwards from there. Perhaps one of the really bad ideas was to open your doors five minutes late every day. That one is sure to upset your clientele. Try flipping it and maybe you'll find that by opening the doors five minutes early, your early bird customers will be pleased that they don't have to wait outside. Hopefully, by compiling the worst-case scenarios, you get a better perspective on what the best-case scenarios are and work from there.

Idea Mapping — This technique has us literally mapping out our ideas on paper in order to make better connections between them. Start with a blank piece of paper. In the center of the page, write your goal or theme for the project. Using the auto shop example from above, let's say our goal is to have a "Successfully Marketed Advertising Campaign." Circle it. Around the circle, write everything you can think of that is related to that goal. Let's say our first set of ideas looks like this: Quality Graphic Design Work, Target Audience Reached, Services Accurately Communicated, and New Customers Gained. Now go through each of these categories and write everything that comes to mind related to them. So, for "Reach Target Audience" let's write: "Identify the Target Audience," "Find Best Advertising Medium," "Appeal to Audience's Sensibilities." Keep this process going for each thought or category you have. For "Find Best Ad Medium," we could write "television," "Local Paper," "Billboards."

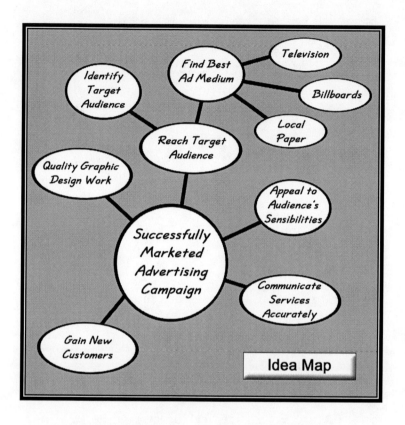

Once you have filled your page with thoughts and ideas, step back and look for connections. Can you find categories that overlap or are mutually beneficial? Perhaps you'll find potential synergies you hadn't recognized before. Draw lines that connect common or related ideas and describe the connection between them.

You'll be left with a map that visually represents the variables you need to manage in order to achieve your goal. Moving forward, you can then pull from all of these elements, prioritize them, and put them in linear order, which becomes your working action plan when set against a timeline. To be sure, you'll reject many of the ideas on the map. You may find that you're able to skip entire steps thanks to synergies from other areas making their purposes obsolete.

Idea mapping can be used many different ways. Instead of having a goal as the center of your map, it could be a problem to solve or an opportunity to evaluate. You can also use mapping to focus on a particular task, using the technique to map out every element necessary to accomplish the task.

Six Thinking Hats – This technique offers a way to structure your analytical process while searching for new and innovative ways to solve a problem. It's based on the premise that we have a tendency to employ our individual problem solving abilities out of concert with the others. One moment we bring healthy skepticism to a proposed idea; the next we are optimistic about certain possibilities within it; meanwhile, we haven't taken time to think creatively about expanding the idea or finding new ones. What is potentially lost is a *full* exploration of your skepticism, optimism, and creativity. This technique is all about knowing and structuring your thinking process to maximize the productivity of each of your analytical abilities.

This method is attributed to Dr. Edward de Bono and is explored in his book *Six Thinking Hats*. Each of his hats is given a distinct color, which is used to represent just one step in the analytical process. Participants wearing a certain color hat will only focus on the step, or role, assigned to that hat. By doing this, we recognize the need to employ each step, as it represents a valuable part of our analytical abilities. Here's a list of de Bono's hats, followed by a brief description of their purpose:

❖ White – *Just the facts.* This is the Sergeant Friday approach, "Just the facts, ma'am." Gather as much information as possible while maintaining neutrality on the subject.

❖ Red – *What's my gut telling me?* Listen to your intuition and offer those views without justification or cause. There are no constraints and no logic is required.

❖ Black – *Something's funny here.* Let your skepticism run wild. Bring cold, hard logic with a negative attitude. Show no mercy.

❖ Yellow – *Sunny side up.* Think of every positive aspect of the idea, bringing loads of optimism to the equation. You've eventually got to be logical about the prospects; but before you start, put on your rose-colored glasses.

❖ Green – *Sky's the limit.* Now it's time to get creative. Explore every possibility with the idea. Add or subtract from it. Build new combinations within it. Shape and reshape it. Find new possibilities; money is no object.

❖ Blue – *Who's driving the bus?* The person with the blue hat has to think about the overall process. He or she is the facilitator and is thinking about the thinking that is taking place. The facilitator keeps the process moving, thereby freeing up the other participants to focus on their roles.

There are many ways to put the Six Hats model into practice. You can either use it alone as a way to structure your individual analytical process or in groups. Within the context of a group, you can have everyone wear the same colored hat at once and working with the same frame of mind, or participants can be in different hats at the same time and then switch it up. But there should always be someone driving the bus – someone in the blue hat. This person has to collect the information and direct the process to ensure it stays on track. Oh, and no one really needs to go out and buy different colored hats to force on someone else's head. You could use laminated cardstock to distinguish between the roles. The important thing is to have the roles clearly defined. Give every aspect of the process its proper due.

Atlas of Perspectives — This technique asks the participant to approach a problem from the perspective of someone from a different field. For example, a manufacturing executive trying to solve a supplier problem asks herself, "How would an architect solve this? What about an office manager? A home builder?" By examining methods and resources from other professional fields, you may find solutions you would never see from your normal perspective.

Let's go back to the auto shop example from above and use this technique to find some ideas. The shop's owner is trying to create and implement a successful advertising campaign, which will bring in new customers and help win back lost market share. Instead of just looking within the auto shop field for ideas, the owner searches for ideas from outside perspectives.

First, he looks at a successful restaurant owner and sees that she has built relationships with her customers which keep them coming back again and again. Those loyal customers bring their friends, and new business is created. Taking this lesson back to the context of his auto shop, he realizes that his customers aren't being treated with the same kind of warmth or given the personal attention he sees when he visits the restaurant. Perhaps he could create strong word-of-mouth advertising by treating his customers with warmth and showing a personal interest in their satisfaction. Next, he considers the success of a clothing retailer who relies heavily on advertising to generate new customers. The retailer promotes its product lines as being the most current, cutting-edge clothes of the day. Applying this to the auto shop, the shop's owner realizes he hasn't advertised the fact that he recently purchased a state-of-the-art, cutting-edge piece of equipment that makes his diagnostic capability exponentially more accurate. Maybe he should focus his advertising campaign on his shop's high-tech capabilities and the benefits those bring to his customers. We'll leave it there, but the possibilities go on and on. With just these two outside perspectives, the shop owner has some new ideas to help grow his business.

The ability to generate good, working ideas is not necessarily a God-given talent. Benjamin Franklin was born with an extraordinary mind, to be sure, but it was his determination to use it that distinguishes him in history. What I encourage you to do is to be just as determined to develop the creative, idea-generating part of your mind. In doing so, you have the greatest potential to base your business decisions on the best ideas and most complete information. One thing I have recognized over the years is that the more you work this creative muscle, the stronger it will become – providing you with a host of better possibilities.

CHAPTER SEVEN

Are You Making Tough Decisions or Making Decisions Tough?

We make decisions every day. Some are subconscious, like which sock to put on first, which hand to hold your keys in, or whether you should start your meal with a bite of peas or potatoes.

The more difficult decisions are those we make consciously. Adding to our anxiety about making a decision is the thought that once we decide on something, we can't undo it. We focus on the effect a decision may have, be that positive or negative.

Some of your most important business decisions will be made before you ever start your business. In fact, choosing a business may be *the* most important business decision you'll make. Will it be the most satisfying, most financially rewarding, and most secure? To answer these questions, you need to focus on yourself and consider what you want and need from the business now and in the future. In the planning phase, you might ask yourself:

- ❖ Is this really what I want to do with my life?
- ❖ How will I feel about my choice twenty years from now?
- ❖ Is this really the business for me?
- ❖ Is this really the industry where my greatest opportunities lie?
- ❖ Do I really want to be an employee, or would I be more satisfied owning the   business?
- ❖ Is this really the city where I want to live? Does it offer the opportunities, lifestyle, and security I'm seeking?
- ❖ Will I be able to grow and expand my capabilities in this business?
- ❖ Will I be able to increase my earning potential as my experience in this business grows?
- ❖ What outside influences might negatively influence my chosen field?
- ❖ Could technology make my field obsolete some day?
- ❖ Is there something about this career path that will keep me from burning out?

At about the same time you're making these business decisions, you'll be making personal decisions and asking yourself:

- ❖ Is this the apartment where I should live?
- ❖ Is this the house I should buy?
- ❖ Is this the car for me?
- ❖ Should I get married?
- ❖ Should I have children?

Many tough decisions involve only one unknown, while others have numerous unknowns. Many tough decisions are straightforward, with the best decision being obvious. Others are complex, presenting multiple variables to be considered and requiring your undivided attention. What keeps many people awake at night is not making a decision, but rather it's the lack of a decision or lack of implementation.

How People Decide

There are times when making a decision seems so daunting that no decision is made. When we can't make a decision, we often resort to guessing, or we make the same decision that others have made in similar circumstances, believing this is easier and likely to provide the same result as going through the process for ourselves.

There are also times when we make uninformed decisions, opting for the safe choice as opposed to the best choice. You know what I mean. Maybe it was a purchase decision. You knew nothing about a product or service you were considering. So, rather than make your decision based on the advantages or quality of one product or service compared to another, you made your choice based on price.

Making a decision based on price alone is common, because price is often incorrectly perceived as an indication of quality. In these situations, most people avoid buying the most expensive option because they want to guard against overpaying or feeling ripped off. They also avoid the least expensive option because they think they'd be buying lesser quality. Instead they choose something in the middle price range. They think they're being conservative and getting the best value. Although price is a relative value scale, many people have been surprised to learn that, often, it has nothing to do with the quality or performance of a product or service. While this middle-of-the-road buying strategy does at least move people to a decision, it can also lead to disappointment.

Then there are people who make decisions without gathering any information. They don't analyze their options or perform due diligence, so they have nothing to guide them toward a good decision. These are the individuals who make decisions with their "gut" or choose to "follow their heart." Once again, they are at least making a decision, but this is another flawed technique that will prevent yielding consistently good decisions.

At the other extreme are the individuals who succumb to "analysis paralysis," where information gathering and analysis take on a life of their own. Those with analysis paralysis can't seem to make any forward progress because they get lost in the details, completely forgetting the need to make a decision. Although analyzing options and considering variables are critical to making a good decision, for some people, analysis becomes the last step they ever reach in the decision-making process, always stopping short of the actual decision. It's as though the only decision they make is to continue analyzing. This indecision can be crippling in a business situation and often leads to greater difficulties than having made a bad decision would have.

Then there are people who make decisions very quickly. They analyze a situation, make a decision, implement, and move on to the next project or concern. While everybody differs in his or her decision-making style, my suggestion is that, in the long term, under-analyzing and making quick gut decisions is no better than over-analyzing and getting trapped in analysis paralysis.

Occasionally, in my business career, I've had to make decisions of such magnitude that the survival of the business was at stake. The right decision could have led to great opportunity for growth and increased profits, but the wrong decision could have led to losing the business altogether. When faced with these critical decisions, don't be afraid or embarrassed to ask for help.

The quality of your decisions can be greatly enhanced by seeking advice from an expert in the field who can guide you more safely to the best decision. To me, experts or consultants are like harbor pilots in seaports. Sea captains, to whom the largest oceangoing freighters are entrusted, navigate the expanse of an ocean, managing the weather and currents during the voyage. Yet, they ask for the expertise of a harbor pilot just outside the jetty. The captain is the master of his vessel, but the harbor pilot knows the unique and constantly changing conditions of local waterways that are too dynamic to chart.

It may seem like a digression, but let's think about why we make decisions in our businesses. As a general rule, we want to enhance or improve the business in some way, to move it forward in growth, capture more market share, and become more competitive or more profitable. On the other hand, we also make decisions to protect or shield our business from competitive threat.

Know What You'll Gain – or Lose

As I said earlier, what keeps most people from making decisions is not the difficulty of the decision itself, but the concern for the outcome. So let's consider what the potential outcomes of a decision might be.

In many instances, people in the process of making decisions see the outcome in terms of "win-lose." If they get it right, they win, and if they get it wrong, they lose. However, some decisions are *neither* right *nor* wrong. In spite of the effort put into gathering the right information and analyzing it thoroughly, there's no effect, no win nor loss. It's a tie. So then, which decisions do we want to make? Do we even want to consider decisions that we know could only end in a loss? Do we really want to invest the time and effort of going through the process if we know the only possible outcome is a tie? We all have better things to do.

So we have some decisions to make about how to make our decisions. The first of those is related to the time and effort you need to invest. Are the time, energy, and expertise that will go into this decision-making process even worth the effort? Is the only outcome a loss or a tie? If it is, your decision should be to pass and focus on other alternatives. The only time you should go through the decision-making process is if you believe the outcome will be positive. By choosing your game, you can play win-tie rather than win, lose, or draw.

Like anyone else, I always wanted to make the right decisions in my business. I wish I could tell you I always succeeded. In spite of your best effort, the unforeseen occasionally takes its toll. I found I made my best decisions by following a logical and rational process and then implementing my plan.

Decision-Making: Step by Step

The first and most important step in any decision-making process is to accurately define the opportunity or problem that exists. Until you can do this and clearly communicate it to everyone involved, there's no reason to proceed. It would be a waste of time, and there's a very good chance the decisions made and the actions taken would be wrong and ineffective.

When you state the problem and what truly needs to be decided, you must be honest with yourself and others. Don't sugarcoat it. Honesty builds the most secure foundation for making a good decision. Stating the issues honestly and accurately will ensure that the problem being addressed is truly *the problem*, as opposed to *a problem* which is easier to accept or resolve.

Second, accurately and honestly describe and evaluate the best possible options that could lead to the best possible decision. This will help you identify the most appropriate alternatives, rather than the easiest alternatives.

Thirdly, the next step in your decision-making process should be to designate a time frame within which a decision will be made. Once you've determined the time frame, divide it into segments for gathering information, using outside consulting services, analyzing, discussing, and then actually making the decision.

For some decisions, you'll be forced to choose one alternative or another, but most decisions offer more alternatives and give you an opportunity to determine which is best. Always allocate part of your time in the research phase for identifying your best alternatives.

When gathering information, use every resource possible. Often, these are people who have been in the same situation and had to make the same decisions for their own businesses. Tap industry sources, especially individuals within your business whose daily lives and future security will be affected by your decision.

Once you've identified the best alternatives and gathered as much information as possible, begin your analysis. Take a logical approach to rank the alternatives from best to worst. The tools I employ most frequently are decision matrices and SWOT (Strengths, Weaknesses, Opportunities, Threats) analysis. Many people are familiar with a simple decision matrix that is nothing more than a piece of paper with a line down the middle from top to bottom. On one side of the centerline there is space to list the advantages of making the decision and on the other side, the disadvantages. A decision matrix also can be as complex as a spreadsheet that lists twenty different products that are being considered for purchase, each with thirty different performance attributes being compared. This multifaceted comparison is certainly more complex, but the steps in the process are the same as for the single piece of paper. My goal in selecting which type of analysis I'll use is to select the one that will most likely help me move to the next step and avoid "analysis paralysis."

SWOT analysis is a very simple technique and could even be constructed as a matrix. In SWOT analysis, you focus on four key areas, one at a time:

- ❖ **Strengths** – What are the advantages, strengths and benefits of making this decision?

❖ **Weaknesses** – What are the weaknesses of the decision being made?

❖ **Opportunities** – What opportunities are available by making this decision?

❖ **Threats** – If I make this decision, what is the potential downside? Or, if I make this decision, how will it reduce threats?

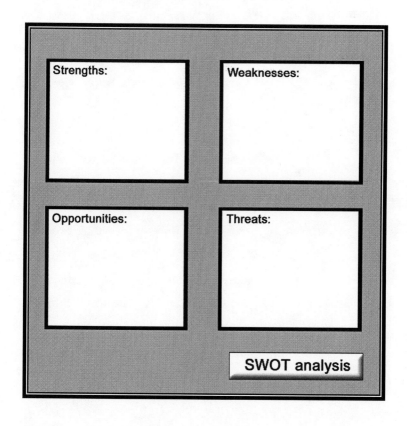

SWOT Analysis: Strengths, Weaknesses, Opportunities, and Threats

Put SWOT to Work for You

Using the grid on the previous page, SWOT analysis could be applied to a business decision. It's very basic, but it demonstrates how valuable this process can be for sorting out details and evaluating their potential effects on your business.

Let's say you're in a customer service business (aren't we all!) You're considering a new piece of equipment that would enable you to expand services to your existing customers and also attract new customers. Using SWOT analysis, let's move step by step through this hypothetical decision.

First, the strengths:

- ❖ Your database allows you to easily communicate with your existing customers.

- ❖ You can sort your database to find current customers who have been pre-qualified as having interest in these additional services.

- ❖ Your business is centrally located and convenient to potential new customers across your entire geographic market area.

- ❖ Your business is well-staffed. Your current employees have the appropriate skill sets, so you could provide these additional services without hiring more employees.

Now, let's take a look at weaknesses:

- ❖ The new technology you're considering could be adopted by others in your market, giving them an edge.

- ❖ Your current facility isn't quite large enough to add the new services without potentially crowding your existing customers and employees.

- ❖ Your company doesn't have a reputation for being innovative.

- ❖ Your business seems to thrive on new customers but has little return business.

As you can see, the strengths and weakness can be, and often are, internal issues. Let's look at the variables that tend to be external – the opportunities and the threats.

Opportunities could be:

- ❖ In addition to attracting new customers, a website presence online could improve the bond between your business and your existing customers.

- ❖ Expanding your services could increase profits.

- ❖ New customers, who are attracted to your business because of your new technology, may transfer all of their business, not just the part associated with the new technology.

❖ Your ability to invest in the new technology may raise the level of your business above competitors in your field.

Threats could be:

❖ Competitors could erode your profit by reducing their prices and therefore your ability to pay for the new equipment.

❖ The technology's performance has not yet been proven.

❖ Competitors have better locations, more work space, and more customer service space.

❖ Additional governmental regulation will burden your business with direct and indirect costs.

Although the SWOT analysis can be a great tool, it can also be very subjective. Keep in mind that SWOT is not a decision-making tool; it's a way of segregating and analyzing the variables involved in making a decision.

Here are a few guidelines to increase the effectiveness of SWOT analysis:

❖ Be brutally honest in acknowledging the strengths and weakness of your business, as well as your market.

❖ After identifying the weaknesses of your business, look for opportunities to eliminate or neutralize them.

❖ Be specific when identifying variables within each of the four areas.

❖ Try to do a SWOT analysis of your competition.

❖ Keep SWOT analysis simple and to the point. Lose the fluff and focus only on the facts.

SWOT analysis is straightforward, simple, and nothing new, but it is a great tool for improving your decision-making process. Like anything else, however, being aware of SWOT analysis, believing in it, and even being able to teach it won't improve your decisions. The only thing that will improve your decisions is to use it.

Now's the Time

Once I reach this stage, I'm ready to make my decision. I've looked at all alternatives and ranked them from best to worst, eliminating those that are ranked the lowest or that I feel are least likely to help me solve my problem. Once I've identified my top two or three alternatives, I review my selection process. There's one more question I ask myself: have I, and those who helped me, been brutally honest in how we described the alternatives, just as we were honest when we described the problem itself? If, after reviewing this information, I believe I have accurately and appropriately considered all the influencing variables, it's time to make the decision.

After the decision is made, you are now ready for implementation. It's my belief that if it's worth my time to put forth the effort to make a decision, then it's a decision worth implementing. To invest all that time and effort without implementation is nothing more than an exercise and a waste of your time and assets.

Implementing Your Decision

Your decision is now made, but this doesn't always mean you're done. When the decision is a straightforward one with a "yes" or "no" answer (do we buy these office chairs?), making the decision ends the issue. Implementation is as easy as buying and sitting in the new chairs. But the decision is often more complicated than that, involving restructuring of some parts of the business. This scenario requires an implementation plan and follow-up. Ironically, putting together an implementation plan presents you with more decisions to make. However, it's worth it in the long run to ensure your decisions deliver their intended effect on your business.

The first step in setting up your implementation plan is choosing what type of implementation you will use. Let's look at four main types of implementation, as named by business writer W. Paul Borkowski:

❖ **The Light Switch Type** – In this type of implementation, the old way of doing things is "switched off" or disabled completely. The new decision is "switched on" or immediately implemented. When you are very confident of the superiority of the decision and it's possible to discard your old system quickly, this is the type of implementation for you.

❖ **The Piece-Meal Type** – This type of implementation introduces the new system in parts over time. This is the right type of implementation to use if you're more confident about some aspects of the decision than others. This also allows you to spread out the cost of implementation for the sake of your budget.

❖ **The Pilot Type** – This type of implementation involves introducing the change only in one section or location of your business. It allows you to work the bugs out or test the feasibility of a change on a small scale before bringing it to the business as a whole.

❖ **The Parallel Type** – This implementation type runs the new system congruently with the old to check its viability and allows employees to get used to it before they have to depend on it. While this is a very secure way to implement a change, there can be extra costs involved with operating two systems at once.

Once you know which type of implementation is right for your situation, you can organize the second part of your implementation plan. This requires laying out what you must have on hand to complete the project. You will need to:

❖ **Define the Objectives** – Clearly state what you want to gain from the project. Visualize what successful implementation will look like.

❖ **Allocate Resources** – Determine and document everything, such as equipment and manpower, that it will take to implement the decision. Make sure you will be able to summon all of these elements easily when you need them.

❖ **Set the Budget** – Calculate the cost of implementation, including possible setbacks, and set aside the funds. Knowing how much you can and should spend on the project will keep costs to a minimum.

❖ **Develop a Timeline** – An organized schedule for implementation will keep everyone involved on task in a prioritized fashion. Also, a defined end date to the project will maintain urgency throughout its execution.

Many large decisions require implementations you simply can't accomplish by yourself. You'll need assistance from your staff or help from outside resources. Another part of your implementation plan is getting your team together. Determine who will be involved in the implementation process. Even though you may have been the original decision-maker, you may not always lead the implementation. Much of the implementation work may be done by your informational technology staff, customer service specialists, or outside contractors. Make sure you have set guidelines for communication between yourself and all of the members of your implementation team.

After implementation is complete, you'll need to do some follow-up work. Set aside time to teach the new system to everyone that will be using it. Set up a meeting with your implementation team to assess the end result. Ask yourselves:

- ❖ Did this transition go as we planned?
- ❖ Are we seeing the results we intended to see?
- ❖ What can this experience teach us about future implementations in the business?

Give honest answers to these questions. If you've made your decision carefully and created and employed a thorough implementation plan, the outcome is most likely to be successful. A decision, once implemented, can yield some unexpected and sometimes unwanted results, no matter how much care was put into the process. Don't become overly attached to your decisions. Your business depends on you to be flexible to stay competitive.

CHAPTER EIGHT
Managing Your Minutes, Saving Your Hours

The first thing you must understand about the concept of time management is that your time is yours and yours alone. Only by you can it be used wisely, given away, or wasted. Although I've written this chapter from a business perspective, you must decide how you will prioritize your time personally *and* professionally. I've found that the people who manage their time best are the ones who approach it not from the standpoint of how they can work themselves and their families into and around their work schedule, but rather how their work schedule can be worked around themselves and their families. It is, however, your choice to make. You must decide where your time will be centered. Will it center on self and family or will it center on work? Choose wisely.

The Neglected Asset

Regardless of how successful or profitable a business is, there's never an endless supply of money. We know our funds are finite, so we pay close attention to budgeting realistically, allocating funds judiciously and projecting our future needs accurately. When the bottom line is in jeopardy, we take whatever steps are necessary to protect it.

There's another critical asset we manage far less attentively, and that's our time. Although we often hear businesspeople complain about not having enough money, perhaps more often, they lament their lack of time: "I wish there were more hours in the day. Where did the time go?" Whether we use our time wisely or foolishly, once spent, it's gone forever. It's history, and there's no getting it back.

Even though time is a finite asset just like money, many businesspeople never think of applying the same principles to both. They don't budget their time, they don't think about allocation, and they don't project their future needs. Yet, when time's up and what should have been accomplished is still undone, the results can be just as devastating as an empty bank account.

Are You Time-starved?

Having enough time is not related to the number of hours in a day, but how we use those hours. Ask yourself these questions:

- ❖ Do you ever feel anxious about all the work you have to do?

- ❖ Are you tired and burned out?

- ❖ Are you pushing important things like family and personal interests farther into the future because too much work has to be done now?

- ❖ Do you procrastinate on important tasks and busy yourself with other "urgencies" that are either fun or easy to complete?

- ❖ Does it seem that everything you have to do is a high priority, leaving you stressed out, feeling unprepared, or constantly under pressure?

Whether you answered yes to one or all of these questions, you can get relief. By appreciating the value of your time and learning how to budget, allocate, and estimate the time you need, you'll reduce some of your anxiety and that sense of being overwhelmed. You'll improve your productivity, as opposed to merely staying busy. You also will turn that tired, burned-out feeling into enthusiasm and excitement. What's more, you'll find time for those important family and personal interests that you've been postponing.

Improving your time management skills will also help eliminate the tendency to procrastinate. You'll be able focus on what's truly important and where your efforts will result in the greatest benefit. I'm very visual when it comes to problem solving or evaluation. The graphic below is an example of the tool that helps me develop a sense of potential benefit relative to effort.

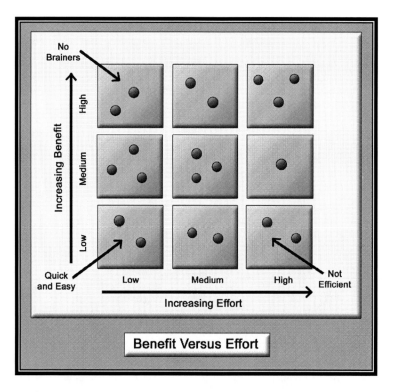

Take Back Control

One of the most important advantages of improving your time management skills and appreciating the value of your time is that you'll get your life back under control. All of a sudden, you'll be able to accomplish more and in less time. You'll gain a better sense of what you need to do first — your high priorities — and what you can delegate or perhaps eliminate from your list.

I want to caution you about trying to solve a time flow problem as you would a cash flow problem, however, particularly if your usual tactic is to try to increase productivity. A business owner who doesn't understand that profit is a function of cost containment as well as sales may think the only solution to a cash flow problem is to ramp up the number of units produced per quarter, month, week, or day, when, in fact, a better solution would be to improve efficiency and cost containment. Merely trying to produce more in less time is a one-dimensional and potentially short-term solution.

The best approach is to focus on better management of the asset (time), better understanding of what tasks need to be completed and better appreciation for the priorities that should exist. Those who are working smarter rather than harder are using their time more efficiently, which brings me to a discussion of the popular time management — or should I say mismanagement — technique called multitasking.

Why Multitasking Won't Save You Time

Many individuals and businesses encourage multitasking. Many believe multitasking can actually be accomplished and that it improves their efficiency and productivity (as well as that of their employees.) In fact, many companies, as part of the hiring process, ask prospective employees if they can multitask.

In my opinion, multitasking just doesn't work.

Have you ever been driving your car and had someone traveling in the opposite direction cross the centerline headed straight at you? After a near collision — and after seeing your life flash before your eyes — you realize he or she was dialing, text messaging, or talking on a cell phone. How many times have you heard of individuals losing control of a car because they looked down to change a CD or turned to talk to someone in the backseat? Do you really think you can read and answer e-mails while you carry on a completely separate conversation on the phone? Multitasking just doesn't work.

Multitasking could not be a more foreign concept to me. All my life, I've had difficulty staying on task without becoming distracted. I have enough trouble paying attention to one conversation, let alone to what's going on across the room at the same time. I have difficulty reading a book because the text makes me think of situations or circumstances in my own life. I have these problems because I have Attention Deficit Disorder (ADD). When I think about multitasking and what people are being asked to do or what people believe they can do, it looks to me like self-inflicted ADD. To me, the effects of ADD and multitasking are the same. You can't do two things at once, so you have difficulty staying on task. The bottom line is that you can do one thing well or try to do two things at once and do neither well.

Multitasking is not the solution to accomplishing more. The solution is better time management. It's not a matter of doing more things simultaneously. It's a matter of how you sequence the tasks, how you prioritize the tasks, and how well you focus on what's important, as opposed to being distracted by things that you might think are urgent, easy to accomplish, or fun to do.

First, Recognize the Need

When I started my business, I'd never heard of the concept of time management. Nobody had ever talked to me about the value of time, only the value of money. Sure, I knew there were things that needed to be done, but at that point in my life, I didn't even make lists. I depended on myself to remember what I needed to do. It didn't take long for me to realize there were so many things going on in my life that I'd never remember everything I needed to accomplish.

My first attempt at time management was to merely make a list of the tasks I needed to complete. I saw my list not as "things to accomplish" but rather "things to not forget." That helped for a short time. It seemed I was getting everything done. Yet, as I began to get busier in my business, there were more demands on my time at work and with my family. I began to get frustrated, anxious, and confused about all of my responsibilities, and I never seemed to get the right things done at the right time. One of my biggest problems was not knowing how to identify which task needed to be finished first.

Generally, I approached my to-do list the way many people do. The things I took care of first were those that happened to catch my attention. And what caught my attention were usually the easy or fun tasks. Admittedly, the things that were fun were typically personal. As a result, my focus tended to be on tasks that were of little or no importance to the business.

I'm not suggesting that personal time and personal duties aren't important. In fact, I think they might be the most important tasks of all. But you'll enjoy them more when you're not feeling guilty about doing them instead of something else that should be a priority. As I began to eliminate my bad habit of focusing on what was easy or fun, I recognized that in doing so, I was prioritizing and assigning value to the items on my list.

Not only is it important to recognize what needs to be done, it's also important to have a process by which you determine the sequence of items to accomplish on your list. Without the proper ordering of items to accomplish, you may experience stress that induces "time crunch" panic.

Don't Panic

The feeling of being crunched for time is one we know all too well. So much is vying for our attention, and so much of it is time-sensitive. We start feeling short of breath. Our hands start shaking. The sense of being overwhelmed robs us of the ability to think clearly. We want to get everything done at once, but panic causes us to freeze.

The origin of the word *panic* gives us insight as to how it should be treated. The roots are in Greek mythology, where one can find the mischievous forest sprite, Pan. According to myth, Pan got his kicks by tormenting travelers as they picked their way through his wooded roads. He would rustle leaves to raise the travelers' apprehension. He would then make spooky noises to frighten the travelers, who would start running. Pan chased them, sounding like a pursuing animal, until they were in such a frenzy that they cut themselves on branches and found themselves hopelessly lost. Our little wood sprite, pleased with himself, would then move on to find the next unwitting band of wayfarers.

In this mythological world, it was the travelers' own perception of danger that got them into trouble. The panic itself caused them to lose their way. If they had only investigated the sounds, they would have found no actual threat.

It's hard to decide which path is the right one to choose when you feel panicked. It's a perfectly human reaction to stress. However, the feeling of panic is extremely detrimental to your business. If you panic whenever you look at your to-do list, you're actions moving forward will more resemble Pan's victims then those of a logical person. Your business will suffer if you find yourself "lost in the woods" whenever you're trying to prioritize your time.

The trick is to create a clear sequence for your to-do list before feelings of panic have the chance to develop. None of us can prioritize proficiently when we're alarmed. Deciding a course of action on the fly can lead to mistakes that will take more time to correct later. For yet another metaphor, remember: a deep-sea diver who panics and heads for the surface too quickly gets the bends.

Decide When an Urgent Matter Isn't

Even though I'd developed a sense of relative importance of one task compared to the next and learned how to avoid panicked prioritizing, my frustration continued because I was still not getting everything done. There seemed to be all these "urgent" things that came up in the course of my day. Either it was the latest crisis or problem to solve, a phone call I had to take, or a deadline I had to meet. In any business, there are truly urgent matters that must be handled as priorities, but for the most part, a lot of what we perceive as urgent is not always important. Likewise, not all-important things are always urgent.

Outside of what I would consider the typical urgencies to which any businessperson must respond, I began to evaluate the other "urgencies" on my list and recognized that they fell into two main categories. In the first category were urgencies that occurred because I hadn't planned ahead or allowed enough time to do something in a timely fashion, for example, the last-minute filing of a quarterly tax return or meeting the deadline for an article due to a professional journal. In the second category were the urgencies I'd "borrowed" from someone else. I took responsibility for these urgencies because the other person hadn't planned or managed his time well. I felt these urgencies were being thrust upon me, when, in fact, they were self-inflicted because I wasn't good at saying no. Taking responsibility for an urgency created by someone else's shortcoming gave me a sense of accomplishment. I took pride in completing these tasks quickly and under difficult circumstances. At the end of the day, however, I realized I hadn't completed the tasks that were important to me, and I felt frustrated, overwhelmed, and unproductive.

I had to learn to say no and feel good about it. This was very hard for me. I wanted to help everyone who asked for my help, but I soon learned there's not enough time in my life to do everything that's important to me *and* handle everyone else's urgencies.

Consistency: The Secret of Time Management

Even though I was making a list, learning how to prioritize and doing a better job of saying no, I was still frustrated. I began seeking information on time management techniques and tools. What I found was very confusing. There were many different time management techniques and just as many different time management tools. Before, I was frustrated because I wasn't familiar with any time management strategies; now I was frustrated because there were so many. I didn't know how to choose what was right for me.

Later, I learned that I started this process like many others before me. I followed one technique for a while, and then I'd change. I'd use one tool for a while, and then I'd change. Although frustrating and not necessarily rewarding, going through that process helped me learn which technique worked best for me and which tool supported that technique. I also recognized that time management techniques and tools had something in common with diets: every single one of them works. Success is just a function of whether or not you use them consistently. You can lose weight on almost any diet, but you can't lose weight if you switch from one diet to another every week. The same is true with time management techniques and tools. Every technique improves your time management; every tool helps you manage your minutes better. Just choose one system and stay with it.

I'm not suggesting that the first time management system you try will be right for you. You'll need to evaluate each one. During your research, you'll learn more about what's available and what best meets your needs. In my experience, it's best to choose your time management technique first and then the tool to support it, rather than try to adapt your technique to the available tools.

Dr. West's Time Management Technique

I'd like to share a simple, yet very powerful time management technique that has served me well for more than twenty years. It has enabled me to accomplish more in less time than I ever imagined possible. You will need a calendar, either paper or electronic, so that you can view details of each day, week, and month.

Begin by making a list of all the tasks that need to be completed, whether business or personal. Now, add one more task and make it number one. This very first task is to take some uninterrupted time to create a list for each and every day. That's right. Creating the list is the number one task on your list every day. You can schedule this time with yourself first thing in the morning or even the night before.

Once you've created your task list, you should review it and decide the order in which the tasks should be accomplished. I recommend that you divide the tasks into three groups: *imperative*, *important*, and *elective*.

The *imperative* tasks are command performances. They are obligatory, and absolutely essential to running your business or personal life. They cannot be overlooked, and they generally have a time constraint or deadline associated with them.

The *important* tasks must be completed because they will have a great impact on your business or personal life. They will influence efficiency, profitability, and improvement within the organization, but they are not as time-critical as the imperative tasks.

The *elective* tasks are those that you can choose to do or not do. Typically, these are things you could do on your personal time or not at all. There are no negative consequences if the elective tasks go undone.

Having divided your tasks into imperative, important, and elective, you may feel somewhat confused about how to proceed when there are several tasks in each category. Here's where you take prioritization to the next level.

Review all of the imperative tasks and identify which one of those is most critical. Assign that task the number one slot, numero uno, the first task to be completed (after making your list, of course). Next, find the second most critical, the third, fourth, and so on.

Apply the same process to the important tasks and to the elective tasks, whether you do them or not.

So you've identified your tasks, determined if they are imperative, important, or elective, and prioritized the tasks within those groups. You now have a planned approach to accomplish your tasks in a prioritized fashion.

Tools You'll Need

The only way your time management tool – your calendar or whatever you choose – can be effective is if you have access to it at all times. If you're always at a computer when making appointments and identifying tasks, then a time management software system may work quite well for you. If you're mobile and on the run all day and choose an electronic system, you'll need a PDA or a smartphone that allows you to schedule tasks and appointments. Or perhaps, for you, a good old, portable, paper time management tool is best.

The other critical part of managing time is remembering to make entries for appointments, meetings, and scheduled phone calls. And don't forget to schedule time for yourself. Perhaps you're working on a project, or you need time to do those things that you prioritized on your task list. Go to your calendar and block time for yourself. That's right; time for you, time to accomplish what you've prioritized. This "self-time" should get the same respect and attention that you give to your most important clients, appointments, meetings, and scheduled calls. When it comes to scheduling self-time, don't shortchange yourself.

Although daily planning is a significant advantage over no planning at all, my ability to be more effective in my daily planning improved as I began to plan long-term, by the week, then by the month, and ultimately by the year. In my practice, my schedule was set a month in advance. I knew when I was seeing patients (for the businessperson, this may compare to having scheduled meetings), when I was doing administrative work, creative work, or project development and when my time was free for myself and family.

Speaking of self, some of the most important time you ever will schedule is your self-time, meaning not only the self-time associated with work, but the self-time for leisure activities or personal and family activities. What I enjoyed most about becoming a better manager of my time is that I recognized it was perfectly okay, and, in fact, *best* to schedule time for myself.

Your Turn

The time management technique I've outlined here is quite simple and basic, but it is also very effective. Will it work for you? That depends.

First, be honest with yourself about what needs to be done and its priority. And second, adhere to that prioritization. If you don't work on the right tasks in the right order, then the task that would most greatly enhance or impact your business may end up going undone.

Although I'm a significantly better manager of my time now than I've ever been, I still can improve. There are times when I get away from my techniques and tools. Those are the times when things go undone or are not done in a timely fashion. At those times, I experience more stress and feel like my life is spinning out of control. Fortunately, those times have become fewer and farther between. I am most productive, most efficient, and least stressed when I employ my techniques and tools every day. The reason is simple: life works better when you budget, project your needs, and allocate your time more wisely.

CHAPTER NINE

Add Value to Your Business by Satisfying Your "Internal" Customers

One of the true keys to success in business — and one that's often overlooked or underappreciated — is developing positive relationships with your employees. Remember, none of us can achieve our goals, in business or in life, without the help of others.

In my practice, I considered my relationships with my employees as though each of them was a bank account. I knew I had to make deposits to these accounts for them to remain sound and function properly. Sometimes my "relationship deposits" took the form of increased pay or bonus compensation. Just as often, these deposits were comprised of encouragement, acknowledgement, and praise.

To appreciate the impact of making regular "deposits" to your relationships with your employees, think about a time when you were on the receiving end of positive recognition. How did you feel? Chances are, you immediately felt better about yourself and were inspired to take your performance to an even higher level, seeking other opportunities for recognition.

Appreciate Your "Internal" Customers

My business was a private optometric practice, providing eye care for patients. In business terms, you could say my patients were my customers. As I gained more insight, however, I realized my business actually had two sets of customers: external and internal. My external customers were my patients; my internal customers were my employees.

Both external and internal customers view the business owner as a resource. Your external customers come to you for service or to solve their problems. Your internal customers — your employees — come to you for compensation. Many employers believe if they pay fair wages, then they've met all of their obligations, and in return, their employees should be willing to provide a high level of service to the customers. In my experience, compensation is only part of the equation.

In my practice, as in any service-related business, we always focused on putting the patients' interests first, and certainly, as far as the medical care we delivered, that was our focus. However, in order to provide the care to patients, I first had to focus on my internal customers. Why is it so critical that your employees are satisfied and motivated? The answer is simple. Your employees can exponentially affect the level of service that people associate with your business and, thus, they have a direct impact on customer satisfaction and the success of your business.

Your Cameo Role as Business Owner

Doctors often believe the only substantive part of a patient's visit is when the patient sees the doctor. And many believe they are the only reason patients return to the practice. In fact, many patients remain loyal to a practice not because of the doctor, but because of the total experience they have when they visit the practice, such as interactions with a key employee or the general attitude of everyone in the practice. In other words, as much as a doctor might like to believe he or she is the center of attention or the main attraction, in reality, he or she may play only a cameo role.

Consider a typical doctor's appointment. Before a patient ever talks to the doctor, an employee schedules the appointment; an employee greets the patient as he enters the practice; an employee interviews him before he sees the doctor; an employee follows up after the doctor's examination, perhaps to educate the patient or collect payment and schedule another appointment.

As this example illustrates, employees in a professional practice (or in any business) who interact with customers have numerous opportunities to enhance the reputation and growth of the practice. Their actions and attitudes will influence whether or not patients will want to stay with the practice and if they feel comfortable referring others. How do you ensure that your employees create this positive experience for your customers?

Every basic business management course emphasizes the need to praise employees. Praise is appropriate at times. However, what many people consider praise actually is encouragement and acknowledgement. There is a difference, and employees respond differently to each.

The Downside of Praise

We've all heard the typical expressions of praise: "Way to go!" "Good job." "You really did well." These comments aren't necessarily bad, but you must be careful to be honest when you deliver praise. For praise to be effective with employees, you also must be willing to identify their shortcomings and communicate them in the same straightforward manner in which you deliver praise.

Remember, too, that everyone is hungry for praise and recognition. Because of that, it's important to avoid using praise to manipulate people. Praise must be genuine, and given for the benefit of the individual who has accomplished something, not because of how their accomplishment benefits you or your business.

Although praise might work in the short run merely because everyone is hungry for approval, it's not something that helps employees grow or motivates them long-term. Praise can turn an employee's attention from the job at hand to merely trying to complete a task so he can receive praise. This change of focus – concentrating on the reward – often results in sub-par work, less initiative, and less insight.

What's more, some individuals can become "praise dependent." Praise becomes their only motivation. These individuals easily lose sight of the importance of the job they perform. Although some people might argue that praise has always worked for them, I think if they take a closer look, they'll realize the "praise" that's been most effective has really been acknowledgement of accomplishments and encouragement to accomplish more.

Acknowledgement Motivates

When you acknowledge, you communicate about a specific behavior, action, or result you observed. For example, you might say, "Gwen, it seems you're always the first one here and the last one to leave." Or you might tell an employee, "It makes people feel special when you remember their names," or "I know that Mr. Johnson is difficult to work with. Even so, you were very patient and understanding during his visit." By acknowledging specifically what you observed, you turn the employee's attention more toward what he or she did than how you reacted to it.

In many businesses, employees earn a base salary, and then, as a result of exceptional performance, they earn bonuses. This additional compensation often has the same effect as praise. If not presented properly, bonuses can begin to look and feel like bribes for special behavior from your employees. I'm not suggesting that you shouldn't offer bonuses, but coupling a bonus with acknowledgement is a more powerful incentive.

Often throughout my business career, a member of my staff would teach me an important lesson about managing a business. It was a staff member who taught me about the necessity of *recognizing* the good work of employees. It happened during our annual performance evaluations.

My approach to annual reviews was different from most. While I evaluated my employees' performances and offered recognition and recommendations, I also asked them to evaluate *my* performance and offer recognition and recommendations to me. The way I looked at it, all of us were there to do a job, and each job was as important to the success of the business as the next. The better we performed individually, the better we performed as a team, the more we all enjoyed what we did, and the better we were all compensated. So, in my reviews, I'd first discuss the areas where I felt an employee had excelled. I'd review their accomplishments during the past year and acknowledge any new responsibilities they'd accepted or skill sets they'd gained. Then it was the employee's turn to evaluate me.

Now, I know what you're thinking: big deal. Who would dare give his employer a bad review? For this approach to be successful, you must make it safe for an employee to honestly tell you, without fear of repercussion, how you've done and where you could improve. It's a matter of creating an environment of mutual trust and respect. This environment doesn't exist just because you *say* it exists. Your actions and the way you communicate with your employees over time create that safe environment.

Cathy had worked in our industry for several years in another city. She had demonstrated a strong work ethic, was a great communicator, and was rightfully very confident in her abilities. I had completed my review of Cathy's performance, which was very positive. In closing, I challenged Cathy to accept some additional clinical and training responsibilities, and I discussed an increase in her base salary. Now, it was her turn to review my performance.

After mentioning some of the management decisions I'd made and acknowledging the positive effects they'd had on the business, she turned to an area where she felt I had an opportunity to improve my performance and my relationships with individual employees. Cathy went on to say that while I was good at praising individual employees and the staff as a whole, I typically did so during the weekly staff meetings and by then my comments, although positive, were rather general. Cathy acknowledged that I was good about saying thank you, but generally I didn't elaborate on the specific tasks that an employee had completed or call out what it was that specifically impressed me.

Cathy's recommendations were simple. I should continue to say thank you and provide my general comments in our weekly staff meetings. In addition, she suggested that I positively reinforce each employee's performance upon completion of a task by commenting on the specific tactics employed and the approach taken for the satisfactory completion of the task. In closing, Cathy said, "Dr. West, everyone appreciates an increase in salary as an acknowledgement of a job well done, but in many ways, expressing your appreciation, letting us know how much our performance makes a difference can be even more important." Lesson learned.

Encourage Participation

One of the most effective ways to acknowledge employees for their abilities and accomplishments and to encourage them to take greater responsibility within the business is to include them in making decisions about how the business should be managed and what, if any, policies should be in place.

To facilitate this in my practice, we had weekly meetings run by the staff. The doctors (or owners) were not allowed to set the agenda or facilitate the meeting. Instead, one employee, selected on a rotating basis, created the agenda and facilitated the meeting. The purpose of setting up staff or office meetings in this manner is to acknowledge the value of your employees' expertise, skill, and insights. My employees regularly conceptualized and implemented ideas that I, as the business owner, may never have thought of.

Your willingness to listen to your employees can be more valuable than hiring outside consultants to advise you. Consultants first have to learn about your business before they can make any recommendations. Then, once they've made their recommendations, they leave.

Your employees' consulting advice is beyond comparison. Not only are they trying to make things better for the business and themselves – they know that once their suggestions are implemented, they have to live with them every day.

Applaud the Effort

It's important to focus employees on the effort they put forth and help them recognize that effort is the most important contribution they can make to the business. I would much rather recognize employees with encouragement and acknowledgement, so they can be proud of their performance and what they've learned, than have them feel their only reward is hearing "good job" at the end of a task.

Generally, we praise employees for performance only after successful completion of a project, a task, or an exemplary effort. As a result, praise-hungry employees may get the impression that the only thing you will ever praise is success. I've seen some employees become so focused on receiving praise that they became very clever at staging opportunities to receive praise when their performance didn't warrant it. I've always felt it's more appropriate to acknowledge employees for their effort than to praise them merely for completing a project. For acknowledgement to be valid, however, you must genuinely appreciate the effort, not just the result. Here's a true story from my practice to demonstrate this point.

It was a Wednesday morning, and the topic of discussion in our staff meeting had been finding solutions, rather than talking about problems. After the meeting, we began our busy day seeing patients. In the middle of the afternoon, the copy machine stopped working. Recognizing that the copier had to be operational for us to complete our work that afternoon, one of my employees tried to fix it. Apparently, a paperclip or staple had become jammed in the mechanism, so the employee tried to remove the object using a letter opener. Unfortunately, her efforts were unsuccessful and, in fact, the letter opener damaged the copier drum. After an emergency visit from a service technician and $800 for a new drum, we were up and running again.

At the end of the day, as I was reviewing charts in my private office, the employee who had tried to fix the copier came in, sat down across the desk from me, and began to apologize for having damaged the copy machine. She said that, even though she couldn't do it all at once, if I would take a little bit out of each paycheck for a few months, she would reimburse me for the cost of the drum because she felt responsible for damaging it.

I listened quietly and after she'd finished speaking, I told her there was no way I would accept any money from her for the repair of the copier. I explained that I was proud of her initiative and how she'd focused on solving the problem. I redirected her attention to the fact that she'd done exactly what we'd discussed in the staff meeting that morning. Rather than dwelling on a problem, she had tried to find a solution in an effort to move things forward in the middle of a busy afternoon. I further explained that I didn't feel any punishment was warranted and that she should not feel badly about the result. Instead, I wanted her to feel good, as I did, about the initiative she took to try to solve the problem.

Some of the greatest opportunities for acknowledgement I have had were in letting my staff know that I had enough confidence in them that they did not have to bring every problem to me. I would rather they brought solutions.

Forms of Acknowledgement

As a business owner, how do you react when employees do something impressive? Unfortunately, some employers don't acknowledge good work at all. They assume the performance was a fluke and that it probably won't happen again anyway. Others rationalize that since they're paying their employees, they shouldn't expect any less.

I recommend making a "relationship deposit." Acknowledge an employee's contribution by telling him what you observed. You could say, "You really went the extra mile to see that Mr. Jones was satisfied," or, "Did you notice the smile you put on Mr. Brown's face after his visit?" or, "You came up with an excellent solution to a complex problem. I'm not sure I would have thought of that."

Another approach is to identify the behavior or the performance you observed and then ask the employee some questions about the task or project he completed. By asking questions, you're putting the employee in the role of the speaker and yourself in the role of the active listener. An example of this acknowledgement tactic would be, "What was the hardest thing about learning to use the new equipment?" or, "How did you decide on that approach to solve the problem?"

My goal in acknowledging good performance and encouraging employees was to focus their attention on what a great job they did, rather than on my reaction. The result, and the point at which I felt I had been successful, was when my employees became aware enough that they could recognize their own good performance, take pride in their accomplishments, and want to share that news with others, not boastfully, but rather with a true sense of accomplishment.

Praising employees with "Great job," "Attaboy," or "Awesome performance" is easy. Acknowledging and encouraging performance is much more difficult.

It takes more effort on your part, but the rewards to you and your employees are significantly greater.

While praise will get your employees' attention, acknowledgement and encouragement will move them to action.

CHAPTER TEN

Negotiation

Negotiation is one of the most basic human activities. People often believe that negotiation only takes place on used car lots and district attorneys' offices. But we're constantly negotiating without realizing it. Most planning, whether it's on a large or small scale, is actually negotiating. When you're putting a plan together for dinner with your spouse, you negotiate the terms. Are the two of you cooking or dining out? If you're dining out, where are you going? This is a good definition of negotiation – you're making decisions together, seeking to settle a matter of mutual concern.

Children are masters at this process. They'll negotiate anything, offering good behavior in exchange for what they want. If their first offer is rebuffed, they will counteroffer until all possibilities are exhausted. They will then often resort to crying tactics. (Think of interactions you've heard at the candy isle of a grocery store.)

While it seems to come naturally to the young, you may doubt your negotiation ability from time to time in your professional career. Negotiation is an important and largely untaught skill. However, it just takes resolve and practice to improve your bargaining prowess.

The Discomfort Zone

By the time we're adults, many of us have lost our willingness to negotiate for what we want. Our Western culture is not set up to encourage open bargaining, and we start to experience a certain amount of discomfort over the process (elsewhere, it is culturally acceptable and even often expected.) We are reluctant to discuss money. We don't want to be perceived as pushy or self-centered.

This is unfortunate because negotiation is a process that can solve problems, as well as pave the way for opportunities. Through negotiation, you can work out payment plans, get better deals on necessary goods and services, and create collaborative relationships. When you are uncomfortable with negotiation, you may seek to avoid it and miss out on chances to benefit your business.

The trick to getting comfortable is to know the three rules of good negotiation and practice them regularly. Most negotiation nervousness comes from feeling inept. Armed with knowledge of the process and a few successful experiences, you'll be able to relax in negotiation environments and may even discover (gasp!) that you enjoy it.

What Makes a Good Negotiator?

Negotiators come in different shapes and sizes, but the ones that consistently attain their goals and maintain their business relationships follow a few general rules. They prepare for the negotiation. They communicate with the negotiation participants, and they conduct themselves ethically. When you incorporate these elements of a good negotiator into your bargaining experiences, you will achieve the best results for your business and find collaborative solutions to problems.

Preparation

Besides being a key ingredient in successful negotiation, preparation can ease discomfort with the process. In the theater business, actors are told to alleviate stage fright by preparing as thoroughly as possible for their role. If they are confident they know their part, they don't have to worry about failure, and the anxiety passes.

In the same way, you can alleviate discomfort or stress you feel about a negotiation by preparing completely. If you have considered the negotiation from all sides and done the appropriate research, you can anticipate aspects of the discussion that you might have otherwise found daunting.

So, preparation will give you piece of mind before negotiation. But it will also help you achieve the best outcome for you and your business. Before the negotiation, you should have a working knowledge of not only your goals and concerns but also your opponent's. Keep in mind that sometimes situations come up on the fly. Even if you only have ten minutes to prepare, you should still go through a shortened version of the steps to get ready. Here are six steps for preparing for a negotiation:

Step 1

Decide with whom you are negotiating. At times, you will be one-on-one with the other side, but, especially in business negotiations, you may have more than one person coming to the bargaining table. Try to find out some information about those in attendance. Are they known for an aggressive or laid-back negotiation style? Do they have the authority to settle in the negotiation, or do they answer to someone else? Answering these questions and formulating your own will help you feel more prepared when you meet.

Step 2

Decide what the issues are. The issues in negotiations can be singular or numerous. Make a list and rank them in order of importance to you. Then, decide what the issues might be to the other side. List those in the order you think the other side would prioritize them. Really try to anticipate their concerns. The issue in a negotiation could seem purely monetary to you, but they could be concerned about any number of equally important issues. For example, they could worry about setting a bad precedent within their company or damaging their reputation outside. Money is often one issue, but it is rarely the only issue.

Step 3

Establish the nature of the negotiation. Negotiations are either distributive or integrative. A *distributive* negotiation occurs when there are fixed resources to be distributed between the parties, so that the more one gets, the less the other receives. For example, a buyer is bargaining for a rug at a fair. The last one hundred dollars they're negotiating over will either go to the rug maker or stay in the buyer's pocket, with no regard for a future relationship between the parties.

An *integrative* negotiation occurs when the resources are not perceived as fixed. This type of a negotiation integrates the aims and goals of all the parties into the solution. Now, let's say a buyer and her friend are at the same fair. The buyer wants a set of glasses but does not have quite enough money. The friend decides to make up the difference for the buyer, in exchange for use of the glasses at a fancy dinner party she has planned. This is a win for everyone. The seller of the glasses gets his price, the buyer gets ownership of the glasses, and the friend, for a small amount of money, gets the glasses for a one-time event.

Both negotiation types are right for different occasions, but integrative negotiations can create a wider span of business relationships and expand your creative opportunities.

Step 4

Determine what you want to accomplish. Set goals. "To do well" isn't good enough. It has been empirically proven that negotiators with concise and optimistic goals tend to achieve better results overall. Aspirations will help determine the outer limits of what you will ask for and inspire you to work for the end result. But you should keep your aspirations reasonable enough to be justified, or you may alienate the other side.

A good way to set goals is to distinguish between your wants and your needs. For example, you may desire a three-year contract with a distributor, but you know your businesses really only needs a six-month contract. You'll work toward the three-year contract but accept six months. The difference between the want and the need is your bargaining room.

Try to imagine the other side's wants and needs as well. Knowing the goals and bottom lines of your fellow participants will allow you to anticipate their actions around the bargaining table.

Step 5

Generate possible options for settlement. Before you meet with the other side, have a stable of creative ways to resolve the issue. One of these options could be the most agreeable solution to the problem or could be a building block for another great idea. Use idea generation techniques, and when time allows, brainstorm with others. Don't just plan on having ideas come to you on the spot. The pressure might make your mind go blank.

Step 6

Know when to walk away. No settlement at all is sometimes better than a bad settlement. As part of your preparation, you need to know your best and worst alternatives to a negotiated settlement. What will happen if you can't agree to terms?

If an *impasse* is reached in our six-month contract example from above, your best alternative to a settlement may be to find another distributor. You could find better service and a stronger relationship with a competitor. On the other hand, your worst alternative to a negotiated settlement with your distributor could leave you without products you depend on for your business. Your business could suffer. Weigh your best and worst alternatives to a settlement against each other. This will give you much-needed perspective on the relative importance of the outcome and help you decide when to give up on the negotiations.

Communication

A good negotiator must be a good communicator. This rule is important in almost every aspect of business, but it becomes crucial when you are planning deals and solving problems. You must exchange information clearly and openly to reach the best solutions for your business. Let's look at what communication qualities are most important in negotiation.

Verbal and Nonverbal Skills

Of course, the ability to express yourself verbally is essential in negotiation. You need to be able to articulate your needs. If you are not able to clearly convey why you are asking for something, the individuals on the other side might infer meanings from your actions that you don't intend. In the same way, if you aren't clear in your refusal on certain issues, they may assume your compliance in the matter. This could create ill will down the line when you have to back out of an assumed agreement.

You also have to be able to express your ideas clearly during negotiations. You could have the perfect solution to a problem, but if you can't help them envision the proposal, they may never accept it.

Along with your words, nonverbal communication plays a fundamental role in negotiation. You need to control the messages your body language sends as well. You may be most comfortable sitting with your arms crossed, but as we all know, this is classically read as a closed-off posture. Drumming the table with your fingers is another little tick many of us have. But if you drum your fingers in a negotiation, the other side may feel you are bored and anxious to get the meeting over with. You can undermine your good intentions with the wrong nonverbal communication.

You should also be able to recognize nonverbal cues in others. These cues do not universally translate (some of us are just more comfortable leaned forward on the table), but they can help you gauge the mood of the other side. Finger pointing, table pounding, looking over the rims of glasses, and placing a hand on the back of the neck can all be signs a participant is agitated. Eye rubbing, temple messaging, yawning, and a blank gaze can be signals that a participant is too tired to continue.

Be aware of all of this activity. It can tell you if your proposal has aggravated your opponents; you may want to remind them of the positive aspects of the idea. It can tell you when participants have grown weary of the negotiation. It can even tell you when you're on the right track and can move on to the next point on your agenda.

Active Listening

Good communicators listen as much as they talk. The active listening style discussed in Chapter 5 is the best for negotiation environments. When bargaining, you will need to listen carefully to the other side. You want to catch the nuances of the conversation so you understand the speakers' wants and figure out their needs. Restating sentiments will assure your participants of your continuing attention, and asking clarification questions will secure against misunderstandings that could undercut the negotiation.

Openness

Open communication will serve you well in negotiation. It is important that you approach a negotiating environment with a willingness to include the opposing view in your world. A negotiation where both sides skirt issues and keep a guard up can waste valuable time. It can also prevent you from thinking up mutually beneficial solutions. The other person may have just what you need to solve an issue, but you'll never know if you don't share your problem. Here is a perfect example to illustrate this point, taken from *Getting to Yes*, Roger Fisher and William L. Ury's classic book on negotiation:

Dr. Roland is working on a vaccine to cure a disease in an underprivileged area. Dr. Jones is working on a serum for nerve gas in a war-torn country. The work of both doctors saves lives. Both doctors need around three thousand Ugli oranges, a very rare fruit grown on a small island in the tropics, to synthesize their medicines. But there are only three thousand Ugli oranges from this year's harvest. Both doctors rush to the tiny island to negotiate for the oranges.

The doctors both have a good cause and the same budget. They argue tirelessly with each other to take home the oranges for their work. They cannot split the crop in half; fifteen hundred oranges will do neither any good.

It seems a terrible choice must be made. However, if the doctors opened up to each other, and negotiated instead of arguing, they would discover that Dr. Roland only needs the juice of the oranges, and Dr. Jones only needs the rinds. They could easily share the oranges to create a "win-win" solution. In this example, open communication in a negotiation could save thousands of lives that would otherwise be lost.

While most negotiations are not so dramatic, the example illustrates the importance of openness in bargaining. If you don't share information, you can't know what will fix an issue.

Ethics

The last rule of a good negotiator is to bargain ethically. This means you enter into every negotiation with good faith, make appropriate legal settlements, and avoid dishonest tactics.

Good Faith

Good faith is an abstract term, but it basically means that you're not trying to defraud the other party or trick them out of information you will use against them. Good faith negotiation is just good business. Your professional reputation is at stake every time you go to the negotiation table. If you've abused past participants in negotiations, word will get out. You may eventually find yourself out of bargaining partners all together.

Legality

"Bargaining in the shadow of the law" is a phrase commonly used in negotiation literature. This means, when you are negotiating ethically, that the settlements you come up with are shaped by existing legal rules. Your solution would stand up if scrutinized in court.

There are common law limits on bargaining behavior in almost every state. Laws can limit the extent to which negotiators can deceive each other. For example, most states prosecute specific false claims, like saying a certain horse is four years old when it's actually fifteen. However, many states allow for "puffing," or general opinion statements, like, "This is a great horse." The legal line can sometimes be thin, so it's good to know the rules governing your area.

On top of common law limits, there are often professional and organizational codes of conduct for negotiations. Your industry may have standards regarding the kinds of deals that can be struck. You should always keep the negotiating standards of your industry in mind to avoid sanctions.

Questionable Tactics

When you negotiate ethically, you do not try to manipulate the other side with cheap tricks. The history of negotiation is full of tactics. Some tactics include turning up the heat in a negotiation room or scheduling a meeting right before lunchtime. These make the opposing party uncomfortable and more willing to settle low, just to escape the situation. Some negotiators flinch dramatically at every single offer made to them in order to drive down the expectations of their opponent.

The list of manipulative tactics in negotiation goes on and on. They all undermine good faith and should be avoided.

It's very possible you will find yourself on the receiving end of unethical negotiation tactics at some point. I suggest two approaches. If the tactic is minor, just ignore it. The instigators will eventually stop when they realize they can't get a rise out of you. If the tactic is bad enough, call them out on it. Show them that you know what they're doing, and you're not falling for it. This should take the wind out of their sails pretty quickly, and you can get back to negotiating. If you ever feel the other side is negotiating in bad faith, you must consider walking away from the meeting. You don't want to risk dealing with people who are trying to harm your business.

Moving to the Middle

Once you've done your preparation, honed your communication skills, and planned for ethical behavior, you'll feel ready to negotiate. But there are a few more aspects of negotiation you need to know as you start to bargain.

Give a Little, Take a Little

You know you need to make reasonable requests in a negotiation; nothing ends a bargaining session faster than inflated demands. However, this does not mean that your first bid in a negotiation should be your bottom line.

In negotiation, there is an expectation of give-and-take. The participants presume there will be several rounds of discussion on an issue. Each round will contain concessions until an agreeable settlement is reached. Keep in mind this is not a tactic but a reasonable negotiation practice.

If you start off the session at your bottom line, you have left yourself no bargaining room with which to negotiate. You will still be expected to make concessions in the inevitable give-and-take process. This may force you into a far worse deal than if you'd started out asking for more.

The Zone of Agreement

In negotiation, the participants each have a set of aspirations for the outcome of the process. We cannot all get everything we want, so we search for collaborative solutions and make concessions to reach an agreement. In making concessions, we are trying to reach the *Zone of Agreement* (ZOA).

The ZOA is the common area between two participants' aspirations. For example, you want to sell a piece of equipment for seven thousand dollars, but the least you will take is forty-five hundred for it. The buyer you're negotiating with wants the equipment for as close to zero as they can get, but they are willing to pay up to five thousand. Between your bottom line of forty-five hundred and their top price of five thousand is the ZOA. Somewhere in this five hundred dollar range is the sum that will please both parties. Here is the ZOA demonstrated visually:

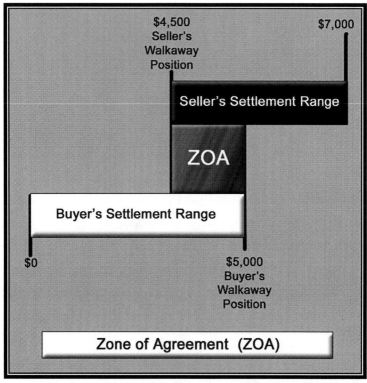

Always look for the ZOA in a negotiation to please both sides and speed up the bargaining process.

A Few Words on Cross-Cultural Bargaining

Just as negotiation styles vary from person to person, they can also vary from culture to culture. In some cultures, there are no fixed prices on merchandise, and negotiation is not only preferred but expected. In other cultures (like our own), there are many situations where an offer to bargain would be considered rude.

As business becomes more and more globalized, you may find yourself entering into negotiations with people from other cultures. Before you begin the process, you should acquaint yourself with the negotiation traditions and rituals surrounding the other participant's culture. Failing to do so will not only appear unfriendly but could cost you in terms of lost opportunities and bad deals.

For example, some of the most misunderstood cultural negotiation rituals involve the consumption of alcohol. In American culture, a rewarding business negotiation is often celebrated after the fact with a toast. But in Japan, heavy drinking is often used to initiate the process. The vulnerability associated with the effects of inebriation is considered a show of trust and commitment to mutually beneficial negotiation. Under these circumstances, if you don't participate in this ritual, the surprised guests may become suspicious of your motives.

Do your homework before a cross-cultural negotiation. Your own cultural instincts may be misunderstood or clash with the traditions of another culture. You want to appear trustworthy and capable to everyone involved. If you are successful at your cross-cultural bargaining, your business could benefit greatly.

CHAPTER ELEVEN

Resolving Conflict
to Gain Opportunities

Just as negotiation is inherent in our lives, so is conflict. Although we may not realize it, our days are full of conflicts large and small. When the alarm wakes you in the morning, you start the internal struggle to get up instead of hitting the snooze button. On the way to work, some jerk cuts you off. While at work, distributors don't deliver, customers are surly, and the computers go offline. At home, the neighbors drive through your flowerbeds, and the kids want to stay out past curfew. All this is in just one day. It may seem overwhelming sometimes, particularly when the conflict involves internal or external aspects of your business. The key to surviving situations like this is strategic, thoughtful conflict management that follows a logical process, accompanied by empathy.

When approached in the right frame of mind, conflict can be just another routine part of doing business, as opposed to the headache and heartache it so often is. This chapter will help you identify your conflict style and offer some advice for solving conflicts, no matter what the size. How you handle disagreement affects how you handle your business; and while it may seem tempting at times to avoid a conflict, this does not solve the underlying issues. If you can move an argument out of a confrontational mode and into a problem-solving mode, you will have gone a long way toward resolution. Maintaining your cool and helping others do the same can be a challenge, but will often benefit you through the development of strong and enduring relationships.

Your Conflict Style

People handle conflict differently. Take an honest look at yourself when you are faced with an argument. Do you like what you see? Does your blood pressure spike and that little vein on the side of your head begin to pulse? Do you shrink from the occasion? Or are you somewhere in between? Everyone adjusts their reactions to conflict depending on the issue and the people involved, but some general trends in your conflict style can emerge when you study yourself. Let's look at the respected work of researchers Kenneth W. Thomas and Ralph H. Kilmann that divides conflict styles into five categories:

The Competitor – These individuals see conflict as a competition. They will argue their positions on an issue to the death, with little regard to the damage being done to their relationships with those on the other side of an issue. A person with this conflict style is uncooperative and only interested in "winning."

The Accommodator – Individuals with this conflict style are unassertive and will quickly abandon their positions on an issue in order to keep the peace. The Accommodators are the "doormats" of conflict.

The Compromiser – People with this conflict style are always looking for the middle ground. They are willing to concede portions of their positions in order to find a mutually acceptable solution to a conflict.

The Collaborator –Those who use this conflict style are willing to devote time and energy to create mutually beneficial solutions to problems. Their efforts are rewarded in that very little of their own positions are compromised while striving to meet the needs of the other.

The Avoider – This conflict style is characterized by dodging disputes altogether. The Avoiders refuse to engage in discussions that could lead to conflict and hope the issues dissipate or get handled by default. The problem with avoiding conflict is that it doesn't go away because you avoid it; it only gets bigger, ultimately more difficult and, in some cases, impossible to resolve.

You may find that you can apply each of these styles from time to time in everyday life. If you need to enforce an unpopular policy in the workplace, you may need to *compete* with a naysayer to achieve decisive action. If your spouse is having a bad day and wants to watch a movie you don't want to see, you'll probably *accommodate* that desire. If you're in a skirmish over the bill at a restaurant, you may *compromise* and split the cost of the meal with your dinner partner. You and a competitor may grapple for clients in a slumping market, but decide to *collaborate* on advertising to attract additional customers to your industry. Lastly, you may choose to *avoid* a confrontation with the person who bumped into you entering the elevator. All of these styles have a valid place, but if you find yourself leaning heavily on one, your conflict management may be out of balance.

What Your Style Communicates

Whichever style of conflict management you employ will send clear messages to your opponent. In every conflict, there's an issue at hand and a relationship at stake (and, yes, you *do* have a relationship with the person who lost your dry cleaning.) If you compete in a conflict, trample your opponent, and view conflict as something to win at all costs, you are demonstrating that the issue is more important to you than your relationship with the opponent. If you accommodate your opponent, you demonstrate that you are willing to concede the issue for the sake of your relationship.

These may not be the messages you wish to convey at all. You may value your relationship with your opponent very much, or the issue may be of dire importance to you. But remember your conflict style, not your intention, *is* sending a message.

Your willingness to compromise and collaborate in a conflict demonstrates your concern for both the issue and the relationship at hand. In compromising, you give some and they give some, splitting the difference so everyone can be moderately satisfied with the outcome. When collaborating to generate the best outcome for all parties involved in a particular conflict, you demonstrate that, while the issue at hand is vital to you, the relationship is held in high esteem and valued going forward.

Avoiding a conflict, although occasionally a good thing, can demonstrate a lack of concern for the issues as well as the relationship between the parties in conflict. If you avoid the conflict, you're communicating that you don't have a strong position on the matter at hand or care about its outcome. You're also saying to the other individuals that your relationship isn't worth protecting; after all, by avoiding the conflict, you have avoided the issues and concerns important to them.

Take a look at the following graph, inspired by the Blake-Mouton Managerial Grid Model and the Thomas-Kilmann Instrument. This graph may help you visualize the balance between concern for the relationship and the concern over the issue at hand. Use this as a thought exercise to help you get a better feel for the way you approach conflict in any given situation.

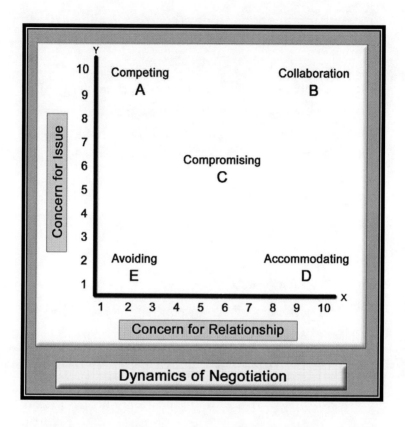

As you can see, at point A the level of concern is high for the issue on the *y* axis, while the level of concern is close to zero relative to the relationship on the *x* axis, indicating the person will compete to win this conflict at all costs. At point B, both the issue and the relationship are of high concern, which lands the person in the section of the graph associated with collaboration. Point C shows a conflict where the issue and the relationship are somewhat important, indicating the likelihood that the conflict will be resolved in some form of compromise. Point D represents great concern for the relationship, while the issue matters very little. This is where you'll see accommodation and concern as a result of regard for the other person. Lastly, point E is representative of someone that shows concern for neither the issue nor the relationship. This person merely avoids or ignores the conflict altogether.

More On Conflict Avoidance

Most of us are averse to conflict, at least to some degree. We're taught from an early age to be agreeable, get along, play nice, and not hurt anyone's feelings (especially in the South.) We carry these lessons from our childhood into our adult lives and professional careers. When a potential conflict presents itself in our lives, we often find ourselves highly motivated to extricate ourselves at all cost. We don't want to appear unfriendly, self-centered, or just plain unlikable. In situations where the source of conflict is inside the office, I've actually seen grown men and women hiding and sneaking out the back door to avoid confronting (or being confronted by) their coworkers. Outside the office, I've known people who have changed their phone numbers or email addresses rather than dealing with a conflict. This is not only ridiculous but also amazingly unproductive and time-consuming behavior. Even if you're not diving under your desk every time a conflict presents itself, minimizing or avoiding conflict may still be negatively impacting decisions you make in your business or personal life. Let's look at several detrimental approaches to dealing with conflict that might develop if you are averse to conflict:

Hiding — As we've already discussed, time and focus are wasted when devoted to deception.

Giving Away the Farm — When faced with direct conflict, some people give in to their opponent's every wish to regain or maintain peace. Later, they regret the agreements reached, and their dissatisfaction with the end result can make them even more averse to conflict in the future.

Stonewalling — Others clam up in conflict; they're present only physically during any debate. They don't participate, in the hopes that their opponent will wear down, give up, and ultimately, go away.

Blowing Up — While this aggressive approach may not initially seem like conflict avoidance, yelling angrily and storming off is clearly not dealing with the issue. Even though this person may initially appear confrontational, ultimately all he has done is removed himself from the argument by burning the bridge the fight was on. It's the grown-up version of "I'm taking my toys and going home."

Lost Opportunities

Conflict avoidance can also create unintentional negatives to your business in the form of missed opportunities. When you avoid interacting with associates, employees, or clients because you fear a conflict, you are also:

❖ **Bypassing a chance to hear their ideas on how to fix the problem.** In fact, their input may be just the outside voices you need to hear on issues concerning your business. Remember, they see things from different points of view, not necessarily the wrong points of view. You could gain valuable knowledge on how to streamline a process or improve customer service. You may learn of an improved technology or the latest empirical data in your field. You don't have to implement everything others say in an attempt at peacemaking, but you'll never know what ideas they have if you don't hear their concerns and ask for their proposed solutions. If you surround yourself with "yes men" (or "yes women") and only hear the positive feedback regarding your products and/or services, you risk stunting the potential growth of your business.

❖ **Missing the possibility of crafting a collaborative solution.** Great partnerships can come from the act of problem-solving together. You and your adversary may actually have complementary holdings, which could only be discovered through in-depth discussion of the issue. Even if a mutually beneficial solution can't be reached at the time of the conflict, maintaining mutual respect and keeping the channels of communication open just might lead to a future relationship.

❖ **Robbing your life of the added color and interest that comes from getting to know others and their perspectives.** Choosing to surround yourself only with like-minded individuals is one of the surest ways to become rigid in your business dealings and static in your personal growth.

Is It Ever Right to Avoid a Conflict?

Despite all I've said about avoiding conflict, there are times when avoiding a conflict is the right move. Here are some examples provided by Thomas and

Kilmann of when it might be appropriate to avoid a conflict:

❖ **When tensions have flared past a productive point.** Sometimes, people really do need to cool off so they can communicate more rationally about the issue at hand, rather than communicate emotionally about the way they feel.

❖ **When you have no chance of winning and you have very little leverage in the situation.** Embroiling yourself in a lawsuit with the federal government over a situation where you know you're wrong would fall into this category.

❖ **When others are more qualified to deal with the issue.** There are times when you need to gracefully step back and let your experts be the experts within an argument.

❖ **When the costs of confronting a problem far outweigh the benefits.** If a person owes you $100 and moves to Uruguay, it may be more cost effective to accept your loss than to plan a trip to South America.

Your own judgment will be your guide here. And as your skills and self-knowledge grow, so will your conflict resolution skills. Remember, you can walk away from some problems, but most will do nothing but fester without proper attention.

The Importance of Conflict Management

If you don't manage conflict well, it may end up managing both you and your business. Negative emotions both in and around a business can snowball, leaving you, your associates, and employees weary, distracted, and frustrated. If you snap at your employees in anger when a problem presents itself, they may hide future problems from you in an effort to avoid the tongue-lashing that accompanies the conflict. This approach and the overflowing behavior that accompanies it can wear away at the fabric of your entire organization. If you're not willing to handle conflicts with your customers promptly and courteously, word will get out that you are hard to deal with. I constantly hear friends vow never to go back to businesses with restrictive return policies. In the worst-case scenario, not being able to resolve an issue with an employee, an associate, or a customer can and does lead to litigation.

Understanding the nature of conflict and developing your ability to resolve it is a vital skill that will aid you in being successful personally as well as in your business.

Positions Versus Interests

Simply put, conflicts are differing viewpoints on the same issue. A discussion participant's viewpoint on a particular issue is considered to be his or her *position*. It's what that person feels is right and the warranted way to deal with the conflict. However, there can be many underlying factors in a participant's position. It's those underlying factors that represent someone's *interests*. You'll be most effective as a conflict manager when you can determine these interests and deal with them.

To use an example, let's say a conflict arises between you and a customer when an appointment is accidentally lost. He is angry. Perhaps he demands to be fit into your schedule and a free consultation. This represents his position. You can try to handle the anger and demands (his position) all day long, but uncovering his interests may provide you insights as to how best to solve the problem. Maybe he feels as though he hasn't received the proper respect or recognition. The oversight makes him feel belittled, as if his business is unimportant to you. Maybe his feelings are hurt because he believes you don't value your relationship with him. Perhaps he is concerned he will be reprimanded at work for taking any more time off to stay longer or reschedule the appointment. This is the bottom line; these are his interests. Any of these interests can be dealt with if they are known. You can assure him that his business and your relationship with him means a great deal to you. You can offer to reschedule the appointment on a Saturday to help him avoid a reprimand at work. None of these solutions would be visible without first discovering his interests.

The Conflict Management Process

We've established that we need to sit down and deal with the interests and the relationships involved in a conflict. But how do you actually go about doing it? Luckily, there are methods for managing conflict. There is one process I find particularly useful, and it's employed by professional negotiators in the field of conflict resolution on a regular basis. This conflict management process has five basic steps that allow people to resolve their disputes. Each step in the conflict management process builds a framework for you to follow when handling a dispute, whether large or small.

Step 1: Getting Together

Many conflicts, like the customer example above, can be worked out quickly by asking questions and actively listening in an effort to identify any underlying interests. It's always best if you can deal with conflicts on the spot. However, other conflicts are more complicated, more emotionally charged, or both. These require you to dedicate a specific time to meet with the other person or people in the dispute, be they associates, employees, or individuals outside your organization.

Consider the setting for your meeting carefully. The venue should be perceived as neutral. The office or home of a participant may put others on the defensive. A third party's office or even the lobby of your building might be a good option. The setting should also be comfortable. It should be clean and clutter-free with adequate seating and easy access to creature comforts. You're not trying to torture the other party!

Choosing your starting time carefully is also important. Setting a meeting at four o'clock on a Friday afternoon could be perceived as inconsiderate and may indicate to the other person that you are not willing invest much time dealing with the issue at hand.

Select your participants wisely and clearly establish who's going to be present at the meeting. Keep your entourage to a minimum and encourage the other side to do the same. Only those directly involved and those authorized to make final decisions are necessary in determining the outcome of a dispute, so it's best to limit attendance to only the "decision-makers."

Step 2: Opening the Meeting

This step of the process consists of both housekeeping and discovery. You'll set the ground rules for the meeting, get to hear the other side's perspective on the conflict, and attempt to neutralize theatrics or dramatic language.

Start by thanking everyone for meeting with you. Remember, by being present, they are demonstrating an interest in moving forward and finding a solution.

Next, acknowledge the difficulty of the situation and commit to respectful behavior during the meeting. Swear off personal attacks, and ask all participants for the same.

Invite your opponents to start by making a brief statement describing their side of the issue and tell them you will do the same. Pay attention while they're talking. Don't smirk, stare off into space, or fiddle with your papers. Make notes, marking where the language is particularly charged. After they have spoken, ask questions for clarification as well as to communicate your interest.

When they are finished, review what they said aloud to indicate your comprehension. Explain that you want to make sure you understand them correctly and paraphrase their statement in neutral language. By neutralizing their wording, you'll give the meeting a more respectful tone. Here's a quick example of paraphrasing in neutral language:

Your Opponent:

You promised me widgets by May, and you lied. Now, I'm out the cash I would have made, and my customers are breathing down my neck!

You:

Let me make sure I'm hearing what you're saying. You feel like the delivery date of the widgets was misrepresented. And now, you feel you've missed economic opportunities and have disappointed your customers.

In this scenario, you have repeated what your opponent said, only you've replaced the emotional language with words that are more professional and calming.

Once you have finished restating your opponent's opening statement, make your own. Keep it brief and talk about the issues, not the people. You are now ready to move on to the next step in the process.

Step 3: Discussing the Issues

This stage of the process allows both sides to discuss the issues in order to create a mutual understanding of the problem. This is where everyone can ask questions and share information to determine the underlying interests associated with the conflict.

Before you go any further, you should set an agenda for the topics to be discussed and decide in what order. Look back at the opening statements and ask the other side for help picking the items on the agenda. These items should be very general and above all, impersonal. Avoid any wording that could be perceived as judgmental.

I believe it's best to begin with the least disputed topics and work up to the most controversial. You should always begin with the easiest topic to give the participants a sense of accomplishment. It will also give you a position to fall back on, in case the going gets rockier as you discuss the more critical issues on the agenda. Here is a sample agenda from the widgets example used above:

1. Relationship — The discussion will include how long the participants have known each other and what business they have done together in the past.

2. Quality of Widgets — This would include past performance issues and previous customer satisfaction.

3. Contract — Here's where the actual terms of the delivery deal are discussed. This is where things may get heated.

4. Economics — Monetary impacts and demands are best kept toward the end of the agenda to prevent participants from getting bogged down in the discussion.

5. Solutions — Every agenda should end with solutions to segue into the negotiating step of the process that follows.

Keep the agenda visible during the meeting to lend structure to this stage of the meeting and to show the participants how much progress is being made. During the meeting, ask open-ended questions to discover the interests of the other individuals involved. Encourage them to ask you questions as well. Volunteer information that helps them understand your interests. This may also be an appropriate time to apologize for any negative impact your actions might have had on them.

During the discussions in this step, keep in mind that when interacting, we're each affected by the mood and behavior of others. Many in the scientific world have even been studying "mirror neurons" in the last ten years, seeking to establish that we are hard-wired to imitate those around us. Scientists believe these "mirror neurons" help us in language development and socialization. Human tendency to imitate each other can be used to your advantage in resolving a conflict. When you remain calm during the discussion of emotional topics and exhibit comfortable, attentive body language, the other side is likely to do the same. If the participants decide to shout, don't escalate the noise level; keep your voice even and respectful while you slow the pace. Eventually, they will begin to mirror your behavior. Remember, if there's going to be any bad behavior, let your opponent provide it. It's much better to have them remember their inappropriate behavior instead of yours.

When you've worked your way down the agenda into the solutions category, you are ready to begin the true negotiation.

Step 4: Negotiating a Solution

This step allows you to start brainstorming about solutions to your problem. Now that you've identified the other side's underlying interests, you can start creating ways to meet each other's needs.

Present what-if scenarios and encourage your opponent to do the same in an effort to consider all possible options for resolution. There's no room for criticism during these brainstorming exercises; they are merely acts of exploration. Make it comfortable for everyone on both sides to freely make suggestions without obligation.

From these possible solutions, both sides should pick the ones that seem most feasible and then brainstorm as to how you might work together and develop them into workable solutions. If a mutually agreeable resolution can be found, you are ready to move on to the next step. If you can't agree on a solution at this point, you need to go back to the drawing board and figure out how best to proceed. There are several options you may decide use. You may be able to negotiate a strategy to sidestep the problem until it can be solved in the future. You can schedule a time to meet again. Or, you may decide to hire a third party such as a mediator to continue working toward a solution. Perhaps as important as anything is to end the meeting on a cooperative and harmonious note, even if the resolution wasn't necessarily what you'd hoped for.

Step 5: Closing the Deal

After you've agreed on a mutually acceptable solution, it's time to hammer out the details and get the points of the agreement down in writing. Don't just walk away from each other after you've decided what might solve your problem. You still need to:

- ❖ Decide on the timetable. A great solution implemented a year too late is no longer a great solution.

- ❖ Delegate the tasks. Make sure everyone at the meeting knows what his or her role in executing the solution is.

- ❖ Schedule a time to reconnect and discuss the progress of the solution. Exchange contact information and let the other side know that you'll make yourself available to discuss anything at anytime.

- ❖ Get your agreement in writing. Everyone involved will be thankful for the clarity that written agreements provide.

When employing this conflict management process, be flexible. Tailor the process to play to your strengths and avoid your weaknesses. Your application of the steps presented here can be at whatever level of formality you feel is appropriate. If at anytime negotiations stall, go back to the last step where you were all in agreement and work forward again. Keep in mind that a solution that benefits both sides is always the best outcome.

Facilitated Conflict Management

If you and your opposition have exhausted all of your efforts in developing a solution to an important conflict by yourselves and want to keep trying, you have the option of hiring a professional. There are several branches within the conflict resolution field. Conflict coaches and consultants are available to visit your business and informally lend a hand. Mediators and facilitative negotiators use a more structured approach to bring the opposing parties together to generate solutions to a problem. Arbitrators decide a case for the parties after hearing both viewpoints. You can even find conflict resolution specialists to conduct a mini-trial to resolve your dispute. All decisions reached at these sessions can be legally binding or non-binding, whichever you prefer. It's up to you to decide whether hiring a professional is right for your business; but it is often a good last option before going to court.

Remember that not all conflicts are solvable. But if you've conducted yourself rationally and explored all of the solution possibilities out there, the other involved party will respect your efforts. Always try to be the person you'd want to deal with in a conflict situation, and the rewards to your career and your personal life will surprise you.

CHAPTER TWELVE

Don't Run From Risk, Manage It

No lessons in business – or life – can be complete without a discussion of risks and risk management. Risks are intrinsic to everything we do. Every time we cross the street or climb behind the wheel of a car, and certainly any time we run a business, we face risks. Some we can control, some we can avoid, and others we have to deal with.

The mere discussion of risks evokes a wide range of emotions, depending on how you deal with them. Some people actually seek risks, some just accept them, some are risk-neutral, and others avoid risks at all costs.

When thinking about business risks, most people think about the potential for reducing the value of the business or losing the business entirely. Losses can result from competition, mismanagement, or financial issues such as solvency or cash flow.

People who are interested in starting their own businesses are most concerned with how much they can invest, how quickly they will get a return on their investment, and whether they can meet their financial responsibilities. People who are considering the purchase of an existing business – which already has a customer base, cash flow, supply chain, and value – have different concerns. They want to know if the company is a good investment, or more appropriately, if the company is a good investment at the given price.

The bottom line is that some degree of risk exists in any purchase or investment. A proactive and conscientious approach to avoiding or minimizing risk can significantly enhance your business success and your financial strength.

Good Risk Versus Bad Risk

Most people associate the word *risk* with only bad outcomes. You've probably heard people say, "I don't want to own my own business because it's too risky. I could lose all my money." The truth is, there are good risks and bad risks. In fact, at some point, you may need to make a choice associated with risk in which the outcome will be good in either instance, just better in one versus the other — a "win-big" versus a "win-bigger" situation. In this situation, losing the potential to be even more successful could be viewed as a loss in the form of a missed opportunity.

Being able to differentiate good risks from bad risks is a function of developing a risk management plan. You need to identify the factors that could negatively impact your business by retarding growth, reducing the value of the business, or wiping out the business altogether. Then devise strategies to manage these risks, while retaining potential opportunities to advance or improve your business.

How you manage risk depends on the type of person you are. Are you a risk-seeker? Do you accept risk? Are you risk-neutral? Do you avoid risk? Regardless of how you would describe yourself, you always have to look at the advantage, or cost versus benefit, associated with each risk, then make a decision and implement it.

Know Your External Risks

Before you can make a cost/benefit analysis about the risks facing your business, you must understand exactly what those risks are. In any business, there are external and internal risk factors. First, let's take a look at some external risk categories:

- ❖ **Compliance** – This type of risk may be related to a business license or professional licensure that allows you to operate your business or provide a specific service. Compliance also may extend to rules, policies, procedures, or expectations set by your industry or by the local, state, or federal government, as well as by customers and the social environment within which your business operates.

- ❖ **Legal** – Every business is bound by legal requirements, such as government-imposed legislation and regulations. Healthcare practices, for example, are subject to standards of care and review by the Healing Arts Board or the Department of Health, and they may be scrutinized by medical facilities that offer privileges to the healthcare professionals affiliated with the practice.

- ❖ **Commercial** – These risks are associated with the market within which your business operates. For example, brick-and-mortar businesses face a commercial risk from Internet commerce. Commercial risks are related to opportunities for you to increase the number of services and/or products that your business can provide within that marketplace. These variables determine your commercial success. You also must consider the viability of a service or product that your business already provides.

Another commercial concern is whether or not the demographics of your geographic market area will provide for the growth of your customer base or the population of people who use your products and services.

❖ **Strategic** – These are risks associated with planning and determining the resources you'll need, not only to establish a new business or to buy an existing business, but also to grow your business. How will you differentiate your products and services from others in the same business in your marketplace? An example of a strategic risk would be launching an advertising campaign to position your business in the marketplace.

❖ **Safety** – Safety can be an external and an internal driver of risk. You must consider the safety of everyone associated with the business, including both your employees and your customers. There are also potential risks with the quality and appropriateness of the products and services your business delivers.

Another risk driver that is both internal and external is the ownership or stakeholder management of the business. If your business is privately owned and you work and manage it, this would be an internal risk. If, however, you have outside investors in your business, the risk could be external as well.

Now Look Inside

Let's turn our attention to some of the internal drivers of risk:

* **Financial** – This encompasses your budgeting requirements and other business obligations, including your ability to pay creditors and manage your accounts receivable. It also relates to cash flow and the liquidity of the business.

* **Organizational** – This involves the business organization, its development, and its behavior. This risk is related to the internal requirements of the business, including the business culture, the organizational structure, and the issues that employees may have that are associated with how the business operates.

❖ **Operational** – This risk driver focuses on the planning and the day-to-day operations of the business, including human resources and any other resources necessary for business growth and the delivery of products and/or services.

❖ **Equipment** – This risk is associated with the equipment used every day to conduct business, whether to fabricate and deliver a product or to provide a service. This includes the general operation and application of the equipment, as well as maintenance, depreciation, safety, and timely upgrades for optimum performance.

❖ **Security** – This risk involves the overall security of a business and its premises, as well as its assets and people. Businesses that have inventory on display, for example, have potential for shrinkage as a result of shoplifting. Other potential risk drivers could be associated with the security of intellectual property, technology, and competitive information.

❖ **Reputation** – This begins with the reputation of the business itself: how the company conducts business, how well the business provides services, and the quality of its products. It also extends to the conduct of the business owner, the employees, and any other individuals who interact with customers or potential customers on behalf of the business.

❖ **Delivery of Service** – These risks encompass not just the delivery of services, but also the quality of the services, the appropriateness of the services to the situations, how products are delivered, and how employees interact with customers before, during, and after a transaction.

❖ **Technology** – This risk relates to the proactive implementation of new technology and how you manage technology within your business. Are you taking advantage of upgrades that would improve the performance of the technology, and are you performing the regular maintenance required for the technology to operate appropriately? This also extends to a business owner's need to recognize and keep up with advances in technology in general and within their industries. There's always a cost/benefit analysis associated with acquiring technology that really exists as part of the business development strategy, as well as the risk-management strategy.

Using the internal and external risk drivers that I've mentioned here, as well as others that might be specific to your business or industry, you can begin evaluating and analyzing your risks to determine their significance and how they might influence the success or failure of your business. By doing so, you will be able to decide whether you should accept, limit, or avoid them.

Analyze Your Risks

Before you can analyze the risks to your business, you must completely understand your market. Risk analysis is more about risks you must manage in the area of opportunity (as opposed to threat.) This involves gathering information about market penetration, geographic boundaries, and the potential for growth in the marketplace. Growth in the marketplace applies to both your local market share and future utilization of your product.

To begin evaluating the risks associated with opportunities to the business, refer to the list of internal and external risk drivers and consider the following activities. Perhaps one of the most commonly used methods for analyzing risk is to brainstorm and imagine various scenarios. This allows you and your advisors to discuss the what-ifs relative to managing threats.

Many of the internal risk drivers of a business can be managed by merely auditing and inspecting everything from how finances are managed to the quality of the product or service delivered. You also can use industry standards to manage internal risks. Most industries make recommendations or set standards for "best practices." To avoid the potential risks of inefficiency, regularly analyze your business processes. If you can improve efficiency, and therefore profitability, by eliminating a process or a step in a process, it's time to make a decision and implement it.

Once you've identified the risks associated with your business, it's important to rank them according to their potential impact. It's also important to recognize that risks can change, thus necessitating an adaptation in your basic business plan. Every business should put a system into place to evaluate and control the consequences of risks, both good and bad.

Manage Your Risks

Once you've identified, evaluated, and analyzed the risks associated with your business, now comes the hard part: dealing with them. Every business has some inherent risks that are beyond control. You may decide to accept them, or if a risk is too high, you may have to accept the change in behavior or the costs associated with mitigating or eliminating them.

Another approach is to transfer at least some of your risk. One of the most common and effective means of doing this is to maintain insurance to protect you from catastrophic events. Once this is in place, you can turn your attention to reducing the day-to-day risks of running the business. You should definitely consider liability insurance to cover you when customers are on your property and while employees are at work; a product liability policy will cover any claims that might arise from product quality or performance. In healthcare, malpractice insurance is a basic necessity.

You may be able to introduce certain processes, systems, policies, or guidelines to help reduce risk within your organization. Although not always possible, the most desirable way to deal with risk is to eliminate it completely.

Risk management is not a one-time event. It's an ongoing process that requires the discipline to focus your attention and effort. Regularly reviewing the status of your risk drivers and addressing and updating your management strategies can significantly enhance the success of the business, as well as your competence in managing it.

Managing What's Beyond Your Control

Many business owners feel that potential threats to their businesses most likely will come from liability circumstances, but there are other situations that pose just as great a threat to the survival of a business.

When I began my practice in 1975, my insurance advisor suggested that disability and business overhead insurance were good investments. I begrudgingly acknowledged that he was the expert, took his advice, and began paying premiums on both these policies. Over the next twenty-seven years, I complained every time I wrote the check for the premiums. That was until the morning I woke up with double vision.

I know it seems ironic that an optometrist would have a vision problem that would prevent him from examining and treating patients, but there I was. The dollars I had invested over twenty-seven years in premiums for business overhead insurance paid great dividends in the months that followed. Because I was a key employee and responsible for well over half the income of the practice, my absence and inability to practice could have been fatal for the business. Instead, the business overhead insurance paid on a regular basis and provided the cash flow necessary to meet payroll and pay the rent, utilities, and other fixed expenses.

By developing a risk management process, you can limit your potential financial losses as a result of the failure of some normal business operation.

Be Aware, Not Afraid

Every business faces risks, but it isn't the risk itself that creates problems. What creates problems is the inability to identify the risk, analyze the risk, categorize the risk, and manage the risk. It's a question of your ability to narrow your focus and attention so that you can systematically evaluate each risk, one at a time.

In my experience, a combination of risk acceptance and risk management is the best way to move a business forward. Risk *avoidance* never seems to work for two primary reasons: 1) you can never avoid all risks; and 2) in attempting to completely avoid risks, you also eliminate a lot of great opportunities.

Chapter Thirteen

The Complacency Plateau

So, now you've got some good tools in your business toolbox. You have a time management plan. You have processes to handle risk, decision-making, idea generation, and conflict resolution. Your internal and external customers are happy. You're enjoying some success. It's time to relax, right? Wrong. There is now another danger stalking your business from within – complacency.

Complacency creeps in when you start to feel like everything in your business is good enough, as opposed to good. You've done the hard work and established the management processes that have put every aspect of your business on rock-solid ground. It feels good to no longer be fighting for the survival of your business, and you begin to drop your guard. It's at this point that many are tempted to kick back, congratulate themselves, and set their businesses on cruise control. Where once they were always searching for ways to improve their operations, now they only get fully involved when a crisis presents itself. They used to drive the business; now they only show up for accidents. If you're this kind of businessperson — always reacting to crises instead of preventing them — where is your business headed? Over the cliff?

Let's extend the driving analogy and consider two things: cruise control and the behavior of novice drivers. Cruise control in automobiles is a great accessory. Some people use it and some don't. However, no one uses cruise control without constantly monitoring traffic and road conditions — at least not without bad results. You've got to keep your eyes on the road, because the road is always changing and always demands your attention. Now think about the novice driver. (If you've ever taught a teenager to drive, this will be easy.) The inexperienced driver has a tendency to drive as though the car will go straight down the road without regular corrections. Consequently, the novice only realizes a steering correction is necessary at the last minute, and an exaggerated jerk of the wheel often follows. Then they overcorrect and must correct the overcorrection; and, in doing that, overcorrect again. In the end, the car is zigzagging down the road from crisis to crisis because the driver is making last minute – and very poor – corrections.

Now put your business, and everything you've worked toward, in the passenger seat of that car. If you've become complacent and "checked out" of the active leadership and management of your business, who *is* behind the wheel? It may be someone who's inexperienced and unqualified to drive. If so, this may explain why you only show up when the car is in the ditch. What happens when you set the cruise control and become distracted by the radio or cell phone? You lose focus on your primary task and might end up in a ditch, too. Either way, these are very uncomfortable rides for everyone involved – and no place for your business to find itself.

As you move along in your career and up the ladder of success, you must take purposeful action all along the way to ensure you reach your ultimate goals. You must remain engaged and vigilant – not just through the start-up of your company, but throughout its life. There is no finish line in business. When you become complacent, you not only fail to achieve new goals but also to see shifts in your industry. This chapter will help you recognize inertia and re-energize your approach to the success of your business.

Where Complacency Lives

Complacency exists in all phases of our lives. People are complacent in their relationships with others and complacent about themselves. Many are even complacent with their health, their finances, their family obligations, their faith, their responsibilities at work, and the list goes on, and on, and on.

With all of this inertia around you, you may even become complacent with complacency. In your business, as in any other aspects of life, complacency breeds complacency. In the worst-case scenario, this leads to failure and, in the best-case scenario, to landing well short of your potential. If you want to garner more success for yourself and ensure the longevity of your business, it's time to make an honest self-assessment of who you are and what your business has become. This will ensure that complacency hasn't quietly crept into what you perceive to be a robust personal life and a growing business with a bright future.

I was once called on by a business owner to advise him on the overall management of his business and, specifically, to assist him in developing a marketing strategy. This particular business had been a family owned, closely held, and tightly managed enterprise for over sixty years. But, recently, the business was shrinking in market share and profitability. After arriving at his business, I began making my initial assessment in an effort to establish where the business currently stood. I interviewed employees and managers before I interviewed the owner. In doing so, I was given the impression that one of the main obstacles to overcome was a very complacent attitude held by most, if not all, of the employees. Most of the employees had been with the company over fifteen years, and a few more than twenty. Recognizing this, I began to collect my thoughts on which suggestions I might make to the owner in my interview with him the following day.

I put together some ideas of what needed to be done to get the employees refocused and interested in growing the business. I was prepared to discuss these ideas, at least casually, right up until I began to interview the owner. What I found in him was an owner who had been so successful for so long that he had become complacent regarding the management of himself, his business, and its employees. I began to recognize that the business and employees were a mirror image of the man I was now interviewing. As we chatted more about the future of his business, I began to recognize an unfortunate and common theme. The employees no longer saw the leader as he once was. Rather, they saw a man who had gotten to the point where he felt immune to competition and unaffected by market trends. He falsely assumed that because he had once been very successful, he always would be. Where there was once a business owner who sought to grow his business by any means possible, there now sat an owner who was satisfied with the status quo, out of touch with his employees and with the business overall. He had become complacent to merely keep things the way they used to be.

In a business sense, all he wanted to do was tread water. The owner didn't want the business to shrink and fail; yet he wasn't interested in leading anymore, growing anymore, supporting his employees in growth and development anymore, or seeking new challenges for himself. He had become complacent and given up on himself, in addition to becoming comfortable with a business that was no longer viable.

As I completed the interview with the owner, he asked me to share some of my observations regarding his business, his employees, and himself. It wasn't easy because what I had to say focused personally on the owner more than his employees or his business.

As I began, I explained the lack of dedication and focus I saw in the attitudes of his employees. Then came the hard part — telling the owner that he was the root of the problem. Upon hearing that, he leaned forward in his chair and moved closer to me. He then began to defend himself with explanations of why he couldn't be the source of the problem. Part of his explanation went like this:

> This business has been in my family for three generations. I myself have been in this business for over thirty years. Most of my employees have been with me over fifteen years. This business is our life.

Now, with the owner red in the face and that small vein throbbing on the side of his head, he listened as I offered my opinion. He needed to turn things around, and a big part of that meant he needed to refocus on enhancing his customers' experience. This could be done by improving the attitude and dedication of the employees and beginning a fresh marketing campaign to ignite and sustain the growth of the business.

That's when he said it. The owner, still leaning forward with the vein throbbing angrily, said, "I'm not interested in growing the business; I've done that all my life. I want you to tell me how to maintain the business as it is currently. Am I asking too much just wanting to keep the business as it is? Can that be so hard?"

My response set him back in the chair with his arms hanging loosely at his sides. I said, "It's not only hard; it's impossible. I can show you how to grow a business, and I can show you how to kill a business, but I have no idea how to merely keep a business the same. In my experience, businesses are either growing or dying. Even businesses that seem to be static are actually ones their owners are attempting to grow, just not successfully." He stared. "I know you don't want to kill your business, and I'm willing to help you grow you business, but if you're looking for someone to advise you on how to keep your business the same, I'm not the one. In fact, what you're asking me to do is be complacent in my advisory role similar to the way you've been in your role as the owner, and that wouldn't be a pleasant experience for you, your employees, nor me."

The owner and I ended up parting on good terms, each appreciating (yet perhaps not understanding) the other's position. The business closed its doors sixteen months later, and the owner went to work for a competitor in the same industry. So ended a sixty-year-old business and the investment of time and talent from three generations of owners and employees. There were no headlines in the local paper, no flashes on the six o'clock news – the business silently passed out of existence. This was just one of many businesses that have fallen victim to complacency. But it is perhaps the one I had been closest to, not only as a consultant for three days, but also as a patron for over seven years. I'm never in a hardware store that I don't think of this story and the people in it.

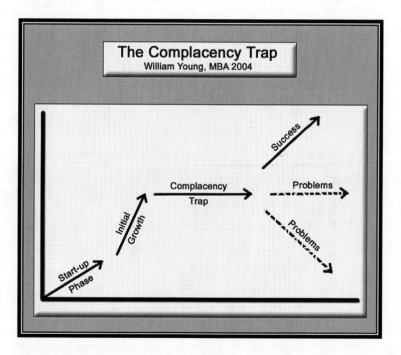

Recognizing Complacency in Yourself

Complacency in yourself is perhaps the most difficult weakness to diagnose. If you're working hard, getting your bills paid, and enjoying some of the finer things in life, you may not notice the subtle changes that signal your performance is lacking. Your approaches to policies, strategies, and tactics which brought you to this level of success are very likely not going to be the ones that will get you to the next level of success personally or in your business. They also may not be the right ones to sustain you in the future. There is nothing constant about success. It is not an absolute, and it's not a destination. Being successful requires that you be flexible and recognize that success is in the journey, in the doing and not in the ultimate reaching of a goal. Interestingly, the satisfaction and the fun are also in the doing; we just never seem to recognize it until we're looking back.

To guard against complacency in yourself, an honest and ongoing self-assessment is necessary. You might begin your self-assessment by asking yourself some general questions such as these:

- ❖ Do I feel I am doing the most I can to maximize my market share?
- ❖ Do I meet or exceed customer expectations every time?
- ❖ Am I keeping up with advances in my field?
- ❖ Am I regularly monitoring my competition?

❖ Am I actively planning for changes in the industry and my company's future?

❖ Are my customers and competitors saying positive things about my business?

With this inquiry, you're looking for any indication of self-satisfaction, strong feelings of security, or even invincibility. If you enthusiastically answered "yes" to any one of these questions above, I encourage you to evaluate this area more closely to ensure that your enthusiasm is warranted. If not, you've identified an area where complacency may already exist in your business.

Digging Deeper

Are you really putting the same level of energy into your business now as you did during its start - up? Have you found yourself saying "no" to customer requests more often? Are you still reading trade journals and actively seeking knowledge as you did at the beginning of your career? How many times a year are you testing your performance against your closest competition? Do you know if there's technology on the horizon that could render your services obsolete? It's up to you as the business owner to realize that there's always more that can be evaluated, monitored, and enhanced. As you identify areas of complacency in yourself or your business, think of it as having uncovered an opportunity to refocus your efforts and increase your success.

I'm not saying you shouldn't enjoy your prosperity. Go ahead, take a vacation. Taking time for yourself will recharge your batteries, sharpen your focus, and actually help you avoid the complacency that comes with burnout or the burnout that comes with complacency. In fact, some of my best ideas and plans for growth have come to me while on vacation, away from my business and the day-to-day demands on my time. Just remember, when you manage your time well, you shouldn't have to be making up for lost time with your family and friends while you're away or making up for lost time in production at work before or after your vacation. Your focus should be on maintaining the right balance of energy for both your business and your personal life.

Recognizing Complacency in Your Employees

Just as you can become complacent with the level of success your business has attained, so can your employees. Even the best employees can become complacent once there has been a certain level of achievement or advancement in the organization. A self-assessment is a good idea for your employees, just as it is for you. The best way to motivate your employees to complete their own self-assessment is to share the insights you gained from doing it yourself. Accomplishing your self-assessment first, and sharing that you've done so, is an opportunity to lead by example. Remember, the complacency that hinders advancement and growth in any business most often comes from the top.

Most everyone would acknowledge that their employees are the face of their company. Employees can help you set policy and effectively identify and solve problems. If your employees are given the impression that you don't appreciate and act on their recommendations, they may become complacent and not offer any. Your business will then lose them as the sentinels of service they should be. If employees are allowed to become set in their ways, your business will lose the flexibility required to consistently meet the requests of customers. This loss of flexibility is a loss your company simply can't afford. Here are some questions that may help you identify complacency among your employees:

- ❖ Do your employees bring new ideas to the table?

- ❖ Do your employees have interest in expanding their knowledge of the industry?

❖ Do your employees often seem more like cheerleaders for the company than critics?

❖ Are your employees resistant to change?

When employees become complacent, they stop looking for ways to improve current systems or processes. Employees may also begin to believe they know well enough how to maintain the company's level of success without seeking out new information. They become more congratulatory than analytical, and they convince themselves that things are fine just as they currently are. In this environment, it doesn't take long before you'll find fresh ideas in short supply and your new ideas and policies met with opposition.

As the owner and leader, you must be able to inspire your employees to reach for higher goals. You must also caution them about the effect that their self-satisfied attitudes can have on the business. It's your responsibility to ensure that your employees appreciate the urgency of the business. Your future, and the futures of your employees, depend on a fresh, dynamic organization, with room for both cheerleaders and dissenters.

Recognizing Complacency in Your Industry

Like an individual business, entire industries can become complacent after experiencing a level of success. They begin to think of themselves as irreplaceable. Old ways become entrenched or even become the standards in the industry. Entire industries can and have been taken to their knees as the result of one innovative and more efficient company from within their own ranks.

The American automobile industry serves as a great example of an industry that lost touch with its market. It obviously needed to streamline its manufacturing process and product offering. The companies never planned on becoming outmoded, yet they became complacent with their success. That's when the time was right for a foreign competitor like Toyota to step in. Toyota brought an innovative, lean manufacturing process to the industry and became a major player in a relatively short period of time.

Regardless of how well you manage your own business, complacency in your industry on the whole could negatively affect you. New technologies and possible collaborations can be squelched. Areas of improvement or expansion can be ignored. Research efforts could be abandoned. The industry overall could earn a bad reputation due to its self-satisfaction and arrogance. Here are some questions to help you identify complacency within your industry:

- ❖ Does your industry predict crises or just react to them?

- ❖ Have trade conferences and writings become more celebratory than informative?

- ❖ Is the average standard of living for participants becoming visibly grand, perhaps at the expense of others?

- ❖ Does your industry invest in research and product development?

- ❖ Does your industry look outside itself for ideas, or does it have all the answers?

As part of your industry, whichever it might be, you need to consider yourself one of its stewards. An industry needs members willing to jar it out of complacency. Remember Newton's First Law: an object at rest stays at rest until acted upon by another force. If you recognize areas of complacency in your industry or within industry organizations, you might be able to help identify threats and opportunities. And, at the same time, you could become recognized as a thought-leader in your field.

Like the other self-assessments in this book, these critical reviews of yourself, your employees, and your industry for signs of complacency require honesty. It may not be easy to admit that you or those you know have hit a plateau on the journey toward success. The sooner you look for complacency, the sooner you will recognize it. And the sooner you recognize complacency, the sooner you can eliminate it.

Getting Your Mojo Back

Just knowing complacency exists goes a long way toward eliminating it. Once you begin your quest to eliminate complacency in your business, you'll begin to recognize the look and feel of complacency in other individuals, businesses, and industries. The following are some suggestions for identifying and eliminating complacency from your business life.

For Yourself:

- ❖ Do a reality check. Take the time to talk to an unhappy customer. You'll gain a much more accurate perspective on the performance of your business than you would by talking to ten happy ones.

- ❖ Compare your business to the leaders in your industry and others. There's always room to expand. You may not feel like such a big fish when the size of the pond is broadened.

❖ Inspire yourself. Look at old pictures or documents that take you back to the start-up days of your business. Rekindle that drive and desire you had to succeed back then. Also, read a biography of a great businessperson you admire. I bet your hero was never described as complacent.

For Your Employees:

❖ Battle boredom. If the workplace has become routine, find ways to shake it up. Give the employees projects that are interesting and new to them, like organizing a charity drive or sponsoring a sports team.

❖ Set higher goals. If your employees feel self-satisfied because of the high percentage of goals they're accomplishing, maybe the goals aren't presenting enough of a challenge. Clearly communicate the higher level of success you'd like to achieve in your business. Getting your employees on board is the first step to accomplishing any goal in your business.

❖ Engage a variety of speakers. You may regularly have speakers present to your employees from within your industry. Identify speakers from other industries to help your employees recognize and eliminate complacency in their own.

For Your Industry:

- ❖ Speak out on the subject of complacency. Find industry forums where you can express your concerns for the industry's forward momentum. Trade journals, central websites, and popular blogs are opportunities as well.

- ❖ Partner with others in your industry. Other business owners may recognize the same negative effects of complacency. Meet several times a year or communicate via phone or email to keep up with the latest news that affects your field.

- ❖ Explore other fields that you believe have similar opportunities and challenges as yours. Specifically, look for other fields that have already gone through a similar growth arc and study how it was handled.

These are just suggestions, of course. There are as many ways to fight complacency as there are instances of it. Only you will know exactly how to motivate yourself and your employees. Likewise, only through communication and research will you find ways to open your industry's eyes to complacency. Being aware of the dangers associated with complacency will help ensure that you, your business and your industry remain viable for the long haul.

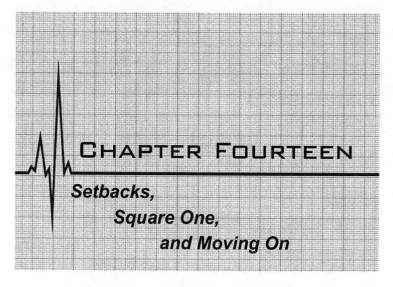

CHAPTER FOURTEEN

Setbacks, Square One, and Moving On

We've all heard the expression "back to square one," and we've probably all used this expression at one time or another to describe a setback or failure in our lives. Have you ever wondered about the origin of the phrase?

One version of the story goes like this. In the early days of radio, BBC announcers were faced with the difficult task of communicating play-by-play action in soccer and rugby. Unlike American football, where the field is divided into ten-yard increments and hash marks, the soccer and rugby fields are marked only at midfield. To allow radio listeners to follow the progress of a game and the movement of the ball, "play grids," as they were called, were printed and distributed throughout the UK. On these play grids, the field was divided into eight squares. As the lead commentator described how a play was developing, a second commentator called out numbers as the ball moved from square to square, thereby allowing listeners to better visualize the action on the field.

The year was 1927, and the first-ever, live radio broadcast of a rugby match was taking place. The ball was put into play, and the usual scrum ensued. The home team was moving the ball downfield when, as a result of an infraction of the rules, play was halted and the ball was returned to its original position on the field. The BBC commentator announced that the ball was going "back to square one." Since that day, the phrase "going back to square one" is used by many and understood by all to indicate a setback of some kind.

Because we all have Square Ones in our lives and because these setbacks can alter or impede our progress, I want to discuss how you can turn an otherwise negative Square One experience into a very positive one. Let's begin by exploring some of circumstances that have sent many of us back to the beginning.

Familiar Square Ones

Career setbacks, such as a change in the market economy, a buyout, a merger, or a technological development that eliminates your job can send you back to Square One.

There are also Financial Square Ones. The stock market, with some regularity, sends people back to Square One. Most recently, the credit crisis and ensuing meltdown of our financial system have put millions of Americans out of jobs, caused the evaporation of trillions of dollars of U.S. wealth, and sent shockwaves of tsunami proportions around the world. That single financial catastrophe created millions of Financial Square Ones, Career Square Ones, and Personal Square Ones almost simultaneously.

Perhaps you've experienced a personal achievement setback, such as a Health Square One, a Weight Loss Square One, a Fitness Square One, or a Personal Growth Square One. Maybe yours is a Personal Relationship Square One in which you must rebuild trust with a friend or family member. And the list goes on. There are Family Square Ones, Aging Parent Square Ones, and Faith Square Ones.

Some people never get out of bed a single day without having at least some part of their lives in a Square One; and everyone has undergone the experience of being back at Square One at least once. Realistically, don't we all expect there will be other Square Ones in our lives? Of course we do.

So, if we've all been in a Square One, and we acknowledge there are more, perhaps many more, Square Ones in our future, then doesn't it make sense that Square Ones are just part of life?

How Do You React?

If Square Ones are a part of each person's life, then being in a Square One at some point isn't all that unusual. The imperative thing while we're there is to not let Square One define us. In this challenging situation, what will define us, what will differentiate us, what will allow us to grow, is the action we take while we're in a Square One. How we react or respond to being in a Square One often has a lot to do with how long we're there and what happens while we're there. Think about how you reacted the last time you found yourself in a Square One. Did you respond with tears, anger, fear, disbelief, denial, self-pity, or withdrawal? Did you blame others, give up, or make excuses? All of these responses are either emotions or outward expressions of emotion. So, let's talk about emotion.

There's much discussion and disagreement about how many emotions there actually are, but for now, I want you to think about only these six in the context of Square One:

- ❖ **Sadness** – Loss is usually associated with setbacks, and sorrow is sure to follow significant loss.

- ❖ **Anger** – We may be angry with ourselves or with someone else – or both – depending on the circumstances.

- ❖ **Fear** – The uncertainties of where we stand and what lies ahead can cause fear in abundance.

- ❖ **Disgust** – It's common to feel disgust while suffering through a setback, particularly if it was caused by someone else or circumstances beyond our control.

These first four emotions are typically considered negative responses to a crisis. They may be stages we must go through while dealing with the fallout, but they don't constitute a positive approach to our new challenges. The next emotion can result in either a positive or negative approach.

- ❖ **Surprise** – The shock of a setback forces these questions upon us: Will we focus our attention on solving the new configuration of challenges? Or, will we crumble into denial, wasting time and resources with old models made irrelevant by the setback?

So, we have four negative emotions and one that can go either way. Now I want to add a positive emotion, one that is hardly ever considered in the context of a setback.

❖ **Happiness** – This is where you're headed. It's why you make the sacrifices and do the hard work. It's the reason you find a way to overcome your anger, sadness, fear, and disgust; and you should always keep your happiness in the front of your mind. Use it to motivate and inspire you while you are struggling with your new challenges.

To have a negative emotional response to a setback is normal and the first part of dealing with a Square One situation. It takes time to get your head around what happened and to consider what the ramifications might be. During that time, it makes sense that your emotions will change based on what you're considering. There are more emotions and emotional responses than I've listed, but in some way, they are all related to these six.

Now, think about these emotions and how effective they would be if they were the only response to a major setback. Will the feelings associated with any of them change the fact that you're in a Square One?

Let's take sadness. Is there anything about being sad that will move you out of Square One? If someone were to ask, "How did you get out of your Square One?", can you imagine yourself answering, "Well, I was just so sad that Square One couldn't hold me. I knew that if I got sad enough, I'd get out?" No, that won't work. You might think of sadness as a motivator, but better yet, eliminating the sadness or seeking happiness is more often the motivator, not the sadness itself.

Now, take anger. Regardless of how angry you get and no matter how that anger consumes you, it won't do a thing to get you out of Square One.

Fear is perhaps the most paralyzing of all emotions. Being afraid keeps many people from getting out of their Square One. In fact, as long as it exists, it can keep someone from even trying.

Disgust, although not particularly crippling, can still keep us in Square One until we deal with and get past it.

Then there's surprise. You know the kind of surprise I mean, the kind that leaves you standing with your mouth open and shaking your head. The amazement, the unexpectedness, and the absolute disbelief grab and hold you until you begin to accept that you really, really are back to Square One.

Think about all of these responses to being in Square One and the emotions associated with them, together with all the others I haven't even named. Will any of the responses and the emotions they represent change the fact that you *are* at Square One? No. The only thing that will move you out of a Square One is action. What you do — and only what you do — in Square One will make a difference.

Own It, Then Take Action

The first thing you must do is assess your Square One objectively. Appraise the circumstances, and see how it feels. Whether you're here because of something you've done, something you haven't, decisions others have made, or outside influences completely beyond your control, you're still back at Square One. There isn't a "not my fault Square One" or a "someone else's fault Square One." There's just a Square One. It's not time to move out of Square One just yet. But it *is* time for action.

I've already discussed the responses and emotions associated with Square One. Perhaps you're thinking I'm going to suggest that you just get past the emotions, but I'm not, at least not yet. The emotions associated with Square One are important. In fact, they're so important that the first action you must take – the first to-do – is to completely explore the emotions you're feeling and how they may affect your approach to getting out of Square One.

Now, think about how you'll turn your emotions around. How will you acknowledge the sadness and disgust? Coming to grips with these two emotions is really a matter of overcoming the denial and, in many cases, the disbelief that most of us experience when we find ourselves in a Square One. How do you turn fear into the courage you need to move forward? How do you redirect the energy consumed by anger into clear thinking and applicable strategy? Ultimately, you want to convert sadness into happiness as you move forward from Square One.

Once you have a clear sense of where you are, it's time to decide where you want to be and what you must accomplish to get there. It's rare for anyone to take that first step from Square One and immediately advance to their goal. I guess it could happen, but I don't think it's ever happened to me. My pathway out of any Square One has always been multifaceted, with the potential to be sent back to Square One just as likely as the opportunity to advance.

Your next step in the assessment phase is to take inventory of what's left. For example, if this is a

Financial Square One and you've experienced a significant loss, you'll want to think about your remaining assets, and whether, going forward, you should focus on being completely conservative. One variable is your age and how soon you'll need the money you lost. Will you need to work longer and retire later, or should you take a more aggressive approach with your investments and try to regain what you've lost? Of course, being too aggressive in your investments might have been what sent you there before. One of the primary areas of focus in your assessment should be about how to advance while guarding against the same sequence of events that put you in Square One in the first place.

Maybe yours is a Career Square One, and as a result of a corporate decision to downsize, your position has been eliminated. You need to take inventory of your skill sets, your experience, and how marketable you are in the same or a similar position with another company. Maybe you're fifty-five years old, and you're actually overqualified for the same position in another company. To move forward, your best course of action is to develop a new set of skills and reinvent yourself in a different industry.

The assessment process in Square One can be humbling. You must be totally, brutally honest with yourself about the good, the bad, and the ugly. And at this point, let me caution you. This is where emotion often creeps back in and compromises your objectivity. This is no time for the rose-colored glasses!

Once you've put the emotions associated with Square One behind you and honestly assessed your abilities and opportunities, it's time to create a vision of where you would like to be. It's important to establish very specific goals and be able to describe them clearly.

In a Financial Square One, for example, you may need to increase the amount of money in your retirement account by 40% within six years. That's a specific goal. You've described your goal in terms of a dollar amount, and assigned a time frame within which you must reach that goal. But there's a lot more to being successful in achieving a goal than just being able to describe it. You have to decide how you'll achieve it, and identify the strategies and tactics you'll use. It's important to focus on your goals, but remember to guard against repeating failed strategies and mistakes.

As you begin your journey from Square One, you must monitor your progress at regular intervals. Regular monitoring of your progress will help ensure that you're moving in the right direction at the right pace. At the same time, you'll start to feel a sense of accomplishment and re-establish confidence in your abilities. Your self-monitoring will be more focused because you're wiser and more aware of the circumstances, situations, and people that could return you to Square One. As you monitor, you may decide to alter your path or pace to protect the new position you've gained. With that alteration, you'll realize that you have newfound wisdom.

Make the Most of Your Visit

Going back to Square One is not all bad. We never seem to appreciate it at the time, but looking back, we often realize we are better off in the long run because of our setbacks.

Perhaps you're better off because of the resolution, planning, and focused action that led to your advancement. Perhaps you were forced to open a new door after the old, familiar one had closed, or you were put in a situation where you had to make a change in your life. Maybe it was a change that you had considered but didn't have the courage to try. At one time or another, in matters large or small, we've all been to Square One and come back stronger, wiser, more aware, more mature, and more successful.

Whether or not you benefit from your visit to Square One depends on what you do while you're there. Many individuals visit Square One over and over and over again. Each time they found themselves there, however, they had more experience to draw from and more insight about the variables they needed to control or manage to move closer to their goal. In other words, each time they found themselves in Square One, they put it to work for them. Ultimately, the accomplishments of these individuals were greater than they ever dreamed possible.

Several visits to Square One also can result in another interesting phenomenon. Sometimes, once the emotions of their setbacks have been explored, people realize their initial goals weren't all they could be. Those goals fell short of what they now recognize they could ultimately achieve.

When I think of individuals who have experienced multiple setbacks to Square One, I'm reminded of the Wright brothers. For years, Orville and Wilbur Wright experienced one setback after another in their quest to help man fly. They regularly found themselves thrown back into Square One until December 17th, 1903, when they changed the world forever with the first powered flight.

Personal Journey to Square One

I also can speak personally about setbacks to Square One. I think all of us can, to some degree. Although I've had many, I'll share one of my most significant Square Ones with you.

On August 15th, 1975, I began practicing optometry. Twenty-seven years and a day later on Friday, August 16th, 2002, I saw my last patient. I didn't realize I'd seen my last patient until the next day, when I woke up with double vision. As a general rule, a sudden onset of double vision is not a good thing. But, fortunately, I soon learned my symptoms were not life-threatening. I would survive, though there was one casualty: my career. Double vision prevented me from examining patients properly. I was done as a practicing optometrist.

Talk about emotion! I was frightened, angry, and frustrated. Everything in my life had always worked out, but this wasn't going to. I began to assess my situation. First, I had to understand my emotions, and I had to take inventory of my skill sets, my experience, what I liked, and what I would do if I could do anything. I had to visualize what I could become. I had to decide on a direction for my life and how I would develop myself. With my experience, I realized I had something to teach about customer care, leadership, motivation, and communication skills. You see, I had practiced optometry, but in doing so, I'd also owned and operated a business. Until this reassessment, I didn't realize I'd developed insights and abilities in each of these areas because I'd always defined myself as an optometrist. This narrow self-description is what initially kept me from seeing the experience and expertise I had in running a business, and in managing and leading people. As I went further with my reassessment, I realized that strong communication skills were the cornerstone of all that I had learned. I'd always enjoyed public speaking and teaching, and I felt this was my calling. Now, six years after my disability presented itself and forever changed the arc of my career, I spend my time doing exactly that – public speaking, teaching, and consulting – all of which I enjoy and find as rewarding as practicing optometry ever was.

There were so many times in my life when Square One gave me an opportunity to reassess, reinvent, and ultimately achieve more than I initially expected that I began thinking that everyone should go back to Square One occasionally. You don't have to give up anything to go back to Square One. You can voluntarily examine your personal life, your career, your finances, or anything else, and decide if you're headed in the direction you truly feel is best for you.

Going back to Square One voluntarily is neither painful nor costly, and it's not as emotional as being put there. Doing so voluntarily is an investment in your future, and I encourage you to make that investment. Going back to Square One could be the most valuable first step you'll ever take.

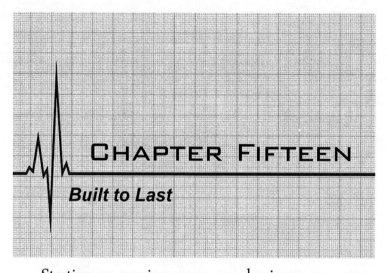

CHAPTER FIFTEEN

Built to Last

Starting or owning your own business can seem daunting. In fact, just the thought of starting or owning a business scares many people into abandoning the idea. Reluctant individuals often cite the failure of other businesses, the cost of start-up, the details they'd have to manage, the work required, a perceived lack of knowledge or training, and the list goes on. In fact, you or someone you know probably has expressed other reasons that I haven't even mentioned.

I've often told a story about an experience I had as a child that seems to come to mind everytime I write or speak on the topic of trying to accomplish something, so let me share it with you here.

When I was five years old, I lived with my family on a cattle ranch in southern Florida. Other than my younger sister, the nearest children to play with were about eight miles away. Because there were no organized activities or playgrounds, I generally entertained myself by playing outside, climbing trees, building roads with my toy trucks, or chasing the cats in the barn.

During the spring and summer, some of the largest grasshoppers I've ever seen made their home in my yard. Now these grasshoppers weren't the little green ones, they were the big, yellow, and black ones with red on their sides that could jump and fly ten to twenty feet at a time. So, it was great sport and quite entertaining to chase them around the yard in an attempt to catch one and put it in a Mason jar. I'd poke holes in the lid of the jar with my pocket knife so the grasshopper could breathe, maybe put a little grass or a flower in the jar to make it feel like home, and I had a friend for the day. I must digress to acknowledge that I realize this makes it sound as though I was very easy to entertain as a child, and I guess I was. In any event, one of the interesting things about those grasshoppers is that they would jump to get out of the jar, even with the lid on, so you could hear this constant thumping sound as their head hit the lid.

One particular day Mom called me in for dinner (the noon meal to most of rural America, not to be confused with supper which is of course the evening meal.). I was allowed to bring my grasshopper into the kitchen, but he couldn't be on the table; so I put the jar with my grasshopper in it on the counter about six feet away, still jumping and still making that thumping sound every time his head hit the lid. I was visiting with Mom, telling her of my adventures that morning when I suddenly realized that I no longer heard the grasshopper's head thumping against the lid of the jar. Fearing the worst, I slowly turned to see if my grasshopper was okay. To my relief, he was still very much alive and quite actively continuing to jump. Interestingly, he had learned just how high he could jump without hitting his head, without it being uncomfortable. I guess you could say he had found his comfort zone.

I suppose the reason I think about my grasshopper when I speak or write on trying is because so many of us behave the same way. We learn just how hard we can try, just how much we can attempt to achieve without it becoming uncomfortable — and there we stop, comfortable and just short of accomplishing what we'd like to, when if we'd persist, stay focused, and push through the discomfort the rewards of accomplishment are just on the other side.

Fear of failure is one of the reasons people avoid starting or owning their own businesses. People don't want to invest their time, talent, and money (or the bank's money), only to lose the investment and feel as though they've wasted their time. Although failure is always a possibility with anything we attempt, the fear of failure in business most often stems from a fear of the unknown.

The idea of starting my own business with no business training or experience frightens me more today than it did in the beginning of my career because now I'm aware of all the things I didn't know that I didn't know. This is why I want to share what I've learned from my failures as well as successes, the risks as well as the rewards, the times I did it right and the times I had to learn from doing it wrong.

Feeling overwhelmed is another reason people avoid starting or owning their own business. There seems to be so much to do. The cash isn't always flowing, and many of the things you do will be for the first time. There's lots of academic business strategy information out there, some of which contradicts itself. It may seem easier to do nothing than to make the first steps.

However, the rewards of crafting a thriving business that gives back to you and your loved ones are way too numerous to give up just because you feel overwhelmed. I understand that making life changes is never easy. The scope of the tasks involved in setting up a new business or reorganizing an existing one can intimidate even the most hardened business owners. The trick is to break down a monumental task into several easier-to-manage pieces.

In much the same way, the idea of implementing all of the points in this book at once would be an overwhelming, if not impossible, undertaking. I suggest taking the book chapter by chapter and prioritizing them according to your needs. Maybe you have time management skills but difficulty negotiating. Maybe you handle conflict well but need help with decision making. Only you know what you need the most work on.

By now, you should have a clear idea of your strengths and weaknesses regarding your business. Self-knowledge and continual self-discovery will allow you to keep the core values of your business strong, while adapting your strategies to the endlessly changing market climate.

This knowledge allowed me to begin my work in 2002 as a business consultant, facilitator, and professional speaker. My new career has taken me across the United States and to sixteen countries on five continents. The insight I provide my clients today is a result of the experience I gained and the lessons I learned throughout my life, and I'm happy now to provide it to you. I hope it will help you all along the way to your goal — creating a successful business that's built to last.